the I Do cookbook for the Bride & Groom

celia jolley . judy williams

Gibson Heritage, LLC
Park City, Utah

Copyright © 2006 by Celia Jolley and Judy Williams

Printed in the United States of America.
All rights reserved. No part of this publication may be reproduced or transmitted in any form or by any means, electronic or mechanical, including photocopying, recording, or any other information storage and retrieval system, without written permission of the publisher.

Gibson Heritage, LLC
Park City, Utah
www.idocook.com

Cover and Interior Design by Linh Jolley
Cover and Food Photographs by Tom Garzand, except: Higginson Photography (page 124 and back cover, cake); Amy Daniels (pages 52, 96, 146, 152, 194, 214, 234, and 314)

A careful effort has been made to verify the source of quotes used in this book.
If any error or omission has occurred, it is completely inadvertent.

Utensils, front cover, courtesy of Amco Houseworks.
Cake topper, page 124 and back cover; Tuxedo cake, page 125,
   © 2003-2006 Wilton Industries - All rights reserved. Used by permission.
Figurine, page 178, Willow Tree ® Susan Lordi. Promise © 2003. Used by permission.

Disclaimer: We have made a conscientious effort to obtain permission from the artists whose works are herein pictured. The origin of some items was impossible to trace. If we have failed to acknowledge your art, we will be pleased to include the information in future editions. Please visit www.idocook.com for contact information.

ISBN 978-0-9792341-0-1

To our mother, Mavis Gibson, one of the greatest of the celebrated "Southern Cooks". Our Mom could create a gourmet meal on a wood stove using nothing but yesterday's leftovers — mixed with imagination and love. Thank you, Mom, for teaching us how to cook. We hope to share your gift with a new generation as they gather to savor the meals and memories served up around the kitchen table. This cookbook is for all who treasure the traditions of home.

Mavis & Ernest 1949

Contents

● Foreword 1

● Wisdom from the
    Red Kitchen Stool 3

● Appetizers & Beverages 4
● Breads 44
● Breakfasts 74
● Cakes & Desserts 106
● Cookies 150
● Main Dishes 186
● Salads 224
● Sandwiches 256
● Sides 276
● Soups 312

● Cooking Helps 344
● Index 367

FOREWORD:

What better way to begin, than with a love story? As young girls, we were fascinated by our parents' romance. For us, it was a thrilling "once upon a time" that began in Stinking Creek, Tennessee. It was 'almost' love at first sight. Dad was a USAAF man who had recently returned from the war, and Mom had just graduated as Valedictorian of her high school class. After the wedding ceremony in June 1946, the two lovebirds built their little nest in the town of LaFollette, Tennessee.

Each day, before Dad left for work, he would go to Mom and give her some goodbye "sugar" (Southern talk for kiss). When it was time for Dad to come home, Mom would comb her hair, freshen up her lipstick and greet Dad with a hug at the door. Riding in the car, Mom and Dad would sing together. We would often request our favorite, *I Don't Want to Set the World on Fire*. The lyrics spoke of two people who did not care about having money or being famous. They only wanted to love each other. It gave us goosebumps when Mom and Dad sang that song, because we could tell they were "in love"!*

Dad fed and clothed his family on a salesman's salary, but Mom deserved much of the credit for our self-reliance. Through her thrift and hard work, she made each dollar count twice. Mom was multi-talented. She wrote songs, painted beautiful soap scenes on the windows at Christmastime, and stitched lovely dresses for her daughters. Each week she planned a menu, prepared a shopping list and cooked meals that usually included half a vegetable garden. Leftovers were never wasted. They were "recycled".

We joined Mom in the kitchen as she taught us the art of cooking. Mom's kitchen was like a Home Economics classroom. All our senses were involved – sight, touch, taste, smell, and sound. It was a home workshop of industry and sociability.

After enjoying a delicious meal there was work to be done, so we washed the dishes, swept the floor, and cleaned the appliances. We learned that for every good thing we enjoyed, there was a price to be paid. Yes, we grumbled! But the message was clear. Blessings demand gratitude, and gratitude is best demonstrated through our actions.

Cooking together not only taught healthy eating habits and housekeeping skills, it served a larger purpose. It was a time we sat on the Red Kitchen Stool while Mom talked to us of the day's events. She listened to our giggles and fears, sang songs, or passed along advice and bits of wisdom.

When our Prince Charming(s) came along, we married them, and then…we cooked! Our children gathered at our tables and ate regular meals and drank their milk, until finally they were all grown up. They are now married and have families of their own. They are honest, hard-working citizens who have pursued higher education, but best of all they enjoy being together. They are loving and caring guardians of the family heritage. We are very pleased with how the "pudding" turned out!

As we raised our children, we were fortunate to have husbands who were good providers. Their labor allowed us to stay home with our children. This is HUGE! Our greatest "thanks" go to our husbands!

We feel strongly that the time-honored traditions of home-cooking and family meals should not become lost in our busy world! These traditions are invaluable as they bring families together to create memories and strengthen bonds of loyalty and friendship.

We owe a heartfelt "thank you" to family, friends, and others who have shared their recipes through the years. We also wish to thank those who have assisted with this cookbook project by sampling the kitchen test results and offering helpful suggestions. Your honesty and patience have made an idea become reality…a legacy of love!

Best Wishes from Celia and Judy

Judy & Celia

*Mom and Dad celebrated a golden wedding anniversary in June 1996 before Dad passed away. Mom tenderly cared for Dad at home during the last years of his life.

'WISDOM' FROM THE RED KITCHEN STOOL:

Old "Wise" Sayings	Interpretation
"The proof is in the pudding."	Pudding must be tended carefully to achieve a quality product. Likewise, relationships require commitment and effort in order to succeed.
"There is more than one way to skin a cat."	Respect your spouse's way of doing things. Different is okay.
"If you keep tapping a horse, he won't know which way to turn."	Nagging causes confusion and discouragement.
"Waste not, want not."	Budget family resources with care.
"Water seeks its own level."	We often choose a partner of like values and talents. We have the power to raise the level of our relationship.
"Charity begins at home."	Save your best self for those you love most.
"You made your bed; now you have to lie in it."	We can choose our actions, but not their consequences.
"You catch more flies with honey than vinegar."	Kindness is more persuasive than criticism.
"Look before you leap."	Weigh the alternatives before making important decisions.
"Beauty is skin deep."	Beauty fades; BE GOOD, not just good-looking!
"Don't cry over spilt milk."	Tears don't change the past, but they can ruin today.
"Don't add insult to injury."	We all make mistakes. Compassion cures the pain.
"Behind every cloud there's a silver lining."	Be optimistic!

Appetizers & beverages

Apple Dip

Artichoke Dip

Cheese Balls

Chicken Chunks

Egg Rolls

Fruit Dips

Guacamole Dip

Lettuce Wraps

Meatballs

Pigs in Blankets

Quesadilla

Salsas

Taco Platter Dip

Veggie Tray and Dip

. . . .

Fruit Shakes

Orange Smoothie

Party Root beer

Rainbow Freeze

Simple Wassail

APPLE DIP

1 cup butterscotch chips
1 (14 ounce) can sweetened condensed milk
½ teaspoon ground cinnamon
6 unpeeled apples, a variety of colors

1. Place butterscotch chips in microwave-safe bowl and microwave uncovered on high until melted. Mix well.
2. Stir in sweetened condensed milk and cinnamon.
3. Return to microwave. Heat until hot but not boiling.
4. Wash, core and slice apples. Serve with dip.

Makes 1½ cups

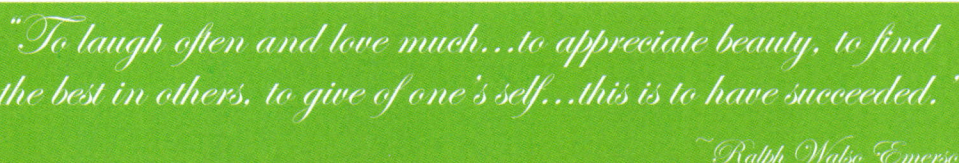

"To laugh often and love much…to appreciate beauty, to find the best in others, to give of one's self…this is to have succeeded."

~Ralph Walso Emerson

ARTICHOKE DIP

1 (8 ounce) package cream cheese, softened
1 (14 ounce) can artichoke hearts, chopped
½ cup mayonnaise
½ cup grated Parmesan cheese
3 tablespoons sliced or slivered almonds

1. Preheat oven to 350 degrees. Grease a small casserole dish (3 cup capacity) or 8" pie plate.
2. Combine cream cheese, artichoke hearts, mayonnaise and Parmesan cheese.
3. Spread in prepared baking dish. Bake 20 minutes or until browned and bubbly.
4. Sprinkle top with almonds and continue baking additional 5 minutes.
5. Serve warm with crackers or raw vegetables.

Makes 2 cups

Spinach Artichoke Dip:
1. Cook 1 cup fresh chopped spinach.
2. Drain excess moisture.
3. Add to Artichoke Dip.

CHEESE BALL

2 (8 ounce) packages cream cheese, softened
½ cup green bell pepper, diced
½ cup onion, diced
¼ cup celery, finely chopped
½ teaspoon seasoned salt
½ teaspoon salt
¼ teaspoon pepper
¾ cup pecans, chopped

1. Thoroughly mix all ingredients, except pecans.
2. Refrigerate until easy to handle.
3. Form into a ball. Roll in chopped pecans.
4. Wrap in plastic wrap and refrigerate several hours.

Makes 1

Serve with assorted snack crackers. A fun appetizer for the holidays!

HEARTY CHEESE BALL

1 (8 ounce) package cream cheese, softened
6 slices deli meat (turkey and/or ham), diced
3 green onions, finely chopped
1½ cups Cheddar Jack cheese, grated

1. Combine cream cheese, deli meat, green onion and ½ cup grated cheese.
2. Form into a ball and roll in remaining 1 cup grated cheese.*
3. Wrap in plastic wrap and refrigerate several hours.

Makes 1

*Substitute chopped nuts.

CHICKEN CHUNKS

3 chicken breast halves, cut into 1" chunks
1 egg, beaten
1 package saltine crackers, finely crushed
½ teaspoon seasoned salt, optional
2 cups oil for deep frying

1. Place chicken chunks into beaten egg and mix. Set aside.
2. Place crackers in plastic food bag and roll with rolling pin (or crush in blender) until crackers are finely crushed. Mix salt into cracker crumbs.
3. With tongs, remove chicken chunks from egg, allowing excess egg to drip off. Roll in cracker mixture until well coated. (Prepare additional eggs and cracker crumbs if they run out before all chicken is coated.) Let prepared chicken chunks sit until oil is heated.
4. In heavy saucepan, heat oil to 350 degrees. Using tongs, carefully place coated chicken chunks into hot oil and fry until chicken is tender and golden brown. Drain on paper towels or other absorbent paper.
5. Serve with choice of dipping sauce.

Serves 4

Sweet and Sour Sauce page 23   Barbecue Sauce page 23

Hot Wing Sauce:
½ cup brown sugar
½ cup red hot cayenne pepper sauce

1. Combine and bring to a boil, while stirring, to dissolve sugar.
2. Serve with chicken chunks or chicken wings.

Mustard Sauce:
¼ cup mayonnaise
1 teaspoon mustard
¼ teaspoon brown steak sauce
1 teaspoon milk
½ teaspoon Worcestershire sauce

1. Combine all ingredients and mix until smooth.
2. Serve with chicken, ham or use as a spread for sandwiches.

EGG ROLLS

2 chicken breast halves, diced*
2 tablespoons sesame oil
1 teaspoon garlic, minced
½ teaspoon ginger, grated
2 cups cabbage, shredded**
2 carrots, shredded**
1 teaspoon sugar
¼ teaspoon salt
2 tablespoons soy sauce
2 teaspoons cornstarch
1 package egg roll wraps
Oil for frying

1. In skillet, stir-fry chicken in sesame oil until tender.
2. Add garlic, ginger, cabbage, and carrots. Stir-fry 3 minutes.
3. Add sugar and salt.
4. Combine soy sauce with cornstarch. Stir into chicken mixture and cook until well blended and slightly thickened.
5. Place about 2 tablespoons mixture in one corner of egg roll wrapper. To roll, follow instructions on package.
6. Deep fry in hot oil (350 degrees) until lightly browned.
7. Serve with sweet and sour sauce, pg. 23, soy sauce or hot mustard.

Makes 18

Substitute cooked pork or omit meat for vegetarian egg rolls

**Substitute packaged coleslaw mix

Leftover egg rolls can be placed in freezer bags and frozen. To serve, reheat in oven, uncovered.

FRUIT DIP

1 (7 ounce) jar marshmallow creme
1 (8 ounce) package cream cheese, softened

1. Combine marshmallow creme and cream cheese. Mix until well blended.
2. Serve with fresh fruit.*

Makes 1½ cups

CREAMY FRUIT DIP

1 (8 ounce) package cream cheese, softened
1 cup powdered sugar

1 teaspoon lemon juice
1 cup whipping cream
¼ cup sugar

1. Mix cream cheese, powdered sugar and lemon juice until creamy.
2. In mixer bowl, whip cream until thick. Add sugar and continue to whip until stiff peaks form.
3. Fold whipped cream into cream cheese mixture.
4. Refrigerate until ready to serve.
5. Serve with fresh fruit.*

Makes 2½ cups

*fresh strawberries, melon, grapes, pineapple or other favorite fruit

Tip: Add two drops pink or green food color if desired.

GUACAMOLE DIP

2 very ripe avocados
1 tablespoon red onion, finely diced
1 tablespoon cilantro, finely diced
½ tomato, diced, optional

¼ jalapeño pepper, finely diced
½ teaspoon salt
2 teaspoons lime or lemon juice

1. Quarter avocados. Remove peel and pit.
2. Thoroughly mash avocado with fork.
3. Add remaining ingredients. Mix well and refrigerate.

Makes 1½ cups

"There is no more lovely, friendly, and charming relationship, communion, or company than a good marriage."
~Martin Luther

LETTUCE WRAPS

1 head iceberg lettuce	1 tablespoon vinegar
2 large chicken breast halves, diced	1 (8 ounce) can water chestnuts
1 teaspoon garlic, minced	2 green onions
½ teaspoon ginger, minced	1 cup fresh mushrooms
2 teaspoons soy sauce	½ (6.75 ounce) package thin rice sticks, optional
1 tablespoon Hoisin sauce	Dipping sauce
1 teaspoon sesame oil	

1. Remove core from lettuce and wash in cold water. Drain.
2. Separate leaves and stack upside down on plate. Refrigerate until very crisp (overnight if possible).
3. In large skillet, stir-fry chicken in 1 tablespoon oil until no longer pink in center. Lower heat to medium. Drain.
4. Stir in garlic, ginger, soy sauce, Hoisin sauce, sesame oil, and vinegar. Cook 3 minutes.
5. Dice water chestnuts, green onions and mushrooms. Stir into chicken mixture and cook until onions begin to wilt.
6. Fry rice sticks according to package directions. Drain on paper towels.
7. To serve, place nest of fried rice sticks on platter. Top with chicken mixture.
8. For each serving, spoon mixture onto crisp lettuce leaf and roll up. Serve with dipping sauce.

Serves 6

Asian Dipping Sauce:

¼ cup sugar
½ cup water
2 tablespoons soy sauce
2 tablespoons rice vinegar
1 tablespoon lemon juice
⅛ teaspoon sesame oil
1 tablespoon hot mustard or brown spicy mustard
2 teaspoons hot water
1 to 2 teaspoons red chili garlic sauce

1. Dissolve sugar in water. Add soy sauce, vinegar, lemon juice and sesame oil. Mix and refrigerate.
2. Mix hot mustard with hot water. Add garlic sauce.
3. Stir into the refrigerated sauce and serve with lettuce wraps.

MEATBALLS

1½ pounds lean ground beef
½ teaspoon black pepper
½ teaspoon salt
½ teaspoon garlic salt
½ teaspoon onion, minced
1 cup crackers, finely crushed, or seasoned bread crumbs
1 egg

1. Preheat oven to 375 degrees. Line cookie sheet with foil.
2. Mix all ingredients. Roll into 1" meatballs and bake 15 to 20 minutes.
3. Serve with barbecue sauce or sweet and sour sauce.

Makes 40

Barbecue Sauce:
1 cup ketchup
¼ cup brown sugar
1 teaspoon minced garlic
1 tablespoon liquid smoke flavor

Combine all ingredients and brush on cooked meatballs. Heat through.

Sweet and Sour Sauce:
½ cup sugar
¼ cup white vinegar
⅔ cup water
2 tablespoons cornstarch
2 tablespoons ketchup

1. Cook sugar, vinegar, water and cornstarch until thickened, stirring constantly.
2. Remove from heat and add ketchup.

PIGS IN BLANKETS

1 (10 count) can biscuits
1 small package smoked cocktail wieners

1. Preheat oven to 350 degrees. Grease cookie sheet.
2. Remove biscuits from can and roll flat. With pizza cutter, cut each biscuit in fourths.
3. Wash and drain wieners. Place each wiener in corner of biscuit piece and roll up so wiener is wrapped in dough. Pinch seam to seal.
4. Place on prepared cookie sheet and bake 15 minutes or until biscuit is golden brown.
5. Serve with dipping sauce of choice.

Makes 40

QUESADILLA

    2 flour tortillas   ½ cup grated cheese
    Butter or oil   Choice of other ingredients*

1. In skillet, heat 2 teaspoons butter or oil over medium heat.
2. Spread butter or oil over one side of one tortilla.
3. Place unbuttered tortilla in skillet on hot oil. Sprinkle cheese over top, plus other ingredients of choice.
4. Top with buttered tortilla, butter side up. When cheese is melted, flip over and brown on other side.
5. Slice in wedges and serve warm.
6. Choice of ingredients can be used to garnish top.

Serves 2

salsa, diced tomato, chopped avocado, thin sliced mango, chopped green onion, diced precooked meat, or sour cream

Note: When adding ingredients, dice or slice very thin and add only small amounts. Quesadilla will not melt together well if too many ingredients are added inside.

SALSA FRESH

[photo page 202]

2 tomatoes, chopped
2 tablespoons onion, diced
2 tablespoons cilantro, diced
½ teaspoon garlic, crushed
½ teaspoon salt, or to taste
¼ small jalapeño, diced*

1. Combine all ingredients well.
2. Chill until flavors are blended and serve cold.

Makes 1½ cups

> *Mild: ¼ small jalapeño
> Medium: ½ small jalapeño
> Hot: 1 whole jalapeño

SALSA

[pictured opposite]

2 tablespoons green chilies, diced
2 tablespoons ripe olives, chopped
1 tablespoon jalapeño, diced
2 large tomatoes, chopped
2 teaspoons red onion, diced
1 tablespoon vinegar
1½ tablespoons olive oil
½ teaspoon garlic, minced
2 tablespoons fresh cilantro, chopped

1. For chunky salsa, combine all ingredients. Refrigerate, covered, until ready to serve.
2. For blended salsa, place all ingredients in food processor and process with blade until desired consistency. Refrigerate, covered, until ready to serve.

Makes 1½ cups

TACO PLATTER DIP

1 (10 ounce) can bean dip, or
   1 (16 ounce) can refried beans
1 cup guacamole
½ cup sour cream
¼ cup mayonnaise
1½ tablespoons taco seasoning mix
½ cup Cheddar cheese, shredded
¼ cup black olives, sliced
½ cup tomato, chopped
2 tablespoons green onion, chopped

1. Spread bean dip or refried beans on 8" or 9" round tray.
2. Spread mild guacamole on beans, leaving about ½" bean mixture showing around edge.
3. Mix sour cream, mayonnaise and taco seasoning. Spread gently over guacamole, leaving edge of guacamole showing.
4. Sprinkle shredded cheese on sour cream mixture.
5. Top with olives, tomatoes and green onions.
6. Refrigerate. Serve with tortilla chips or corn chips.

Serves 6

Mild Guacamole:
2 very ripe avocados
2 teaspoons lime or lemon juice
½ teaspoon salt

1. Quarter avocados. Remove peel and pit.
2. Thoroughly mash avocado with fork.
3. Add juice and salt. Mix well and refrigerate.

Makes 1 cup

VEGGIE TRAY AND DIP

6 large red or green lettuce leaves
½ pound baby carrots
2 celery ribs, cut into thin sticks
1 bell pepper, cut into strips*
1 can black olives, drained

½ cup green olives, drained
10 mini red grape tomatoes
10 mini yellow grape or pear tomatoes
Ranch Dill Dip

1. Wash and drain lettuce leaves. Line 10" tray with them.
2. Arrange carrots, celery sticks, peppers and olives in sections around tray on lettuce leaves.
3. Scatter red and yellow grape or pear tomatoes over black olives.
4. Serve with dip.

Serves 10

green, orange, red or yellow

Substitute or add choice of fresh veggies.

Ranch Dill Dip:
½ cup mayonnaise
½ cup sour cream
½ teaspoon dill weed
1½ tablespoons dry ranch dressing mix

1. Combine all ingredients and chill.
2. Serve with fresh veggies.

Makes 1 cup

FRUIT SHAKE ORANGE

1 cup orange sherbet
½ cup vanilla ice cream
2 cups fresh fruit, chopped*
¼ cup orange juice

1. Combine sherbet, ice cream, fruit and juice in blender. Pulse until fruit is mixed in.
2. Blend until mixture is thick and smooth. Serve immediately.

Serves 2

*banana, strawberries, fresh pineapple, or kiwi

FRUIT SHAKE STRAWBERRY

2 cups vanilla ice cream*
4 large strawberries, sliced
1 banana, cut in chunks
1 tablespoon milk
½ teaspoon vanilla extract

1. Place all ingredients in blender. Pulse until fruit is mixed in.
2. Blend until thick and smooth. Serve immediately.

Serves 2

Variation: Substitute favorite fruits for strawberries and banana.

*Flavored milkshakes: substitute any flavor ice cream and omit fruits.

ORANGE SMOOTHIE

6 ounces frozen orange juice
1 cup milk
½ cup water

½ cup sugar
1 teaspoon vanilla extract
30 ice cubes

1. Combine all ingredients except ice cubes in blender. Blend well.
2. Continue to blend, feeding ice cubes through top of blender until ice cubes are crushed and drink is thick.

Serves 4

"The only true gift is a portion of yourself."

~Ralph Waldo Emerson

PARTY ROOT BEER

4 quarts water
3 cups sugar
4 teaspoons root beer extract
2 pounds dry ice

1. Mix all ingredients, except dry ice, in a punch bowl or large salad bowl.
2. Using a hammer or meat tenderizer, break dry ice into large chunks while it is still in a paper bag. Wear oven mitts to drop the dry ice into the root beer.
3. Stir every five minutes until most of the dry ice is melted. It takes about 30 minutes for root beer to carbonate.
4. Serve immediately.

Makes 1 gallon

RAINBOW FREEZE

1 (12 ounce) can frozen fruit concentrate, thawed*
1 (.23 ounce) unsweetened drink powder**
2 cups sugar
8 cups water
1 (2 liter) bottle lemon-lime soda

1. Mix all ingredients except soda. Place in freezer container and freeze until solid.
2. Take out several hours before serving and thaw partially.
3. Place in punch bowl or large container. Add soda.
4. Break up frozen mixture until drink is slushy.

Serves 20

*limeade, orange juice, pineapple juice, grape juice, cranberry/raspberry or any other favorite frozen concentrate

**Use flavor of powdered drink mix that corresponds with concentrate flavor, such as lemon lime drink mix with limeade, or mix and match favorite flavors.

SIMPLE WASSAIL

2 quarts apple juice or cider
½ cup sugar
1 teaspoon whole cloves
1 teaspoon whole allspice
1 (3") stick cinnamon
½ lemon, sliced thin

1. Combine apple juice and sugar in kettle. Stir.
2. Add cloves, allspice and cinnamon. Boil gently 30 minutes.
3. Remove spices with slotted spoon and discard.
4. Float lemon slices on top.
5. Serve hot.

Makes ½ gallon

"Love is what makes two people sit in the middle of a bench when there is plenty of room at both ends."
~ Anonymous

Breads

Biscuits

Buttermilk Banana
Bread or Muffins

Cheese Biscuits

Cornbread

Dinner Rolls

French Bread
& Breadsticks

Fruit Nut Loaf

Poppy Seed Bread

Potato Rolls

Pumpkin Chocolate Chip
Bread & Muffins

Quick Banana Bread

Scones

Wheat Bread

White Bread

BISCUITS

1 egg, well beaten
1 cup sour cream
1 tablespoon sugar
¼ cup shortening

1½ cups flour
1 teaspoon baking powder
½ teaspoon baking soda
¾ teaspoon salt

1. Preheat oven to 400 degrees. Grease 8"x 8" baking pan (or use cookie sheet and place biscuits 2" apart for a more crisp crust).
2. In a mixing bowl, beat egg with a fork. Mix in sour cream, sugar and shortening.
3. In another bowl, combine flour, baking powder, baking soda and salt. Add gradually to egg mixture. Mix well. Dough will be sticky.
4. Sprinkle a little flour over dough and scoop onto a well-floured board. Handle dough gently.
5. Flour hands and quickly knead dough 4 strokes to form into a ball. Place smooth side up and sprinkle top lightly with flour.
6. Roll gently ¾" to 1" thickness. Cut with 2½" biscuit cutter, dipping cutter in flour with each cut. Place in prepared pan.
7. Bake 15 minutes or until biscuits are golden brown.
8. Serve hot.

Makes 8 biscuits

Buttermilk biscuits: Substitute buttermilk for sour cream and increase flour to 2 cups.

BUTTERMILK BANANA BREAD OR MUFFINS

2 cups sugar
1 cup oil
½ cup sour cream*
1½ teaspoons vanilla extract
1½ teaspoons almond extract
3 eggs
½ cup buttermilk*

4 medium, over ripe bananas
3 cups flour
1½ teaspoons salt
1 teaspoon baking soda
1 teaspoon baking powder
½ cup chopped nuts, optional
Glaze, optional

1. Preheat oven to 350 degrees.
2. Grease and flour 2 (9"x 5") loaf pans or 16 miniature (3½" x 2½") pans. For muffins, grease and flour 2 standard muffin pans or line with paper baking cups.
3. In a large mixing bowl, mix sugar and oil. Stir in sour cream. Add vanilla, almond, eggs and buttermilk. Mix well.
4. Mash bananas with fork and add to sugar mixture.
5. In another bowl, combine flour, salt, soda and baking powder.
6. Gradually stir flour mixture into sugar mixture. Add nuts, if desired.
7. Pour batter into prepared loaf pans and bake approximately 1¼ hours. (For miniature loaves or muffins, fill approximately half full and bake 25 minutes or until lightly brown.)
8. While hot, poke holes in top. Loosen edges and remove from pan. Place loaves on cooling rack set over large cookie sheet. Pour glaze over bread. Cool.

Makes 2 (9"x 5") loaves,
16 miniature loaves or 24 muffins

*Substitute 1 cup buttermilk

Glaze:
1 tablespoon melted butter
½ cup sugar
1 teaspoon vanilla extract
½ teaspoon almond extract
¼ cup orange juice

Mix together and pour over hot bread.

CHEESE BISCUITS

1 cup baking mix*
1/3 cup milk
3/4 cup cheese, shredded
2 tablespoons melted butter
1/4 teaspoon garlic salt, or to taste

1. Preheat oven to 450 degrees. Lightly grease cookie sheet.
2. Combine baking mix, milk and cheese. Stir until well blended.
3. Spoon onto prepared cookie sheet and smooth tops slightly.
4. Bake 8 minutes. Remove from oven.
5. Stir together melted butter and garlic salt. Brush on hot biscuits.
6. Turn oven to broil. Return biscuits to oven for 1½ minutes or until tops are crispy.

Makes 12 biscuits

*Use packaged mix or recipe on Substitutions page 357.

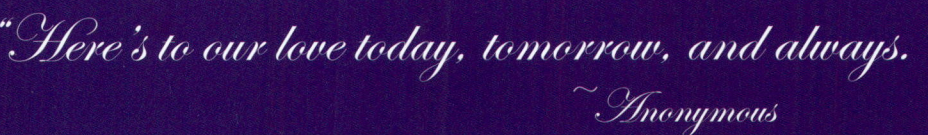

"Here's to our love today, tomorrow, and always."
~ Anonymous

CORNBREAD

1 cup cornmeal
1 cup milk
1 cup flour
3 tablespoons sugar
½ teaspoon salt
1½ teaspoons baking powder
⅓ cup melted butter or oil
1 egg

1. Preheat oven to 375 degrees. Grease 8" square baking pan.
2. In a bowl, combine cornmeal and milk. Allow to soak for 3 minutes.
3. In another bowl, mix flour, sugar, salt and baking powder.
4. Add cornmeal mixture, oil and egg to flour mixture. Stir until all ingredients are just blended. Do not over mix.
5. Spread in prepared pan. Bake 25 minutes or until lightly browned.

Makes 9 squares

Cornbread Muffins: [pictured opposite]
1. Prepare Cornbread recipe.
2. Divide batter between 12 greased muffin cups (standard size muffin pan).
3. Bake about 20 minutes until lightly browned.

Makes 12 muffins

DINNER ROLLS

1 tablespoon yeast
3 tablespoons warm water
1 egg, beaten
2 tablespoons sugar
½ teaspoon salt

3 tablespoons butter, softened
¼ cup hot tap water
¼ cup milk
2¼ cups flour

1. In small bowl, stir yeast into warm water. Let stand until well dissolved, about 5 minutes.
2. In mixer bowl, combine egg, sugar, salt and butter. Stir in hot water. Add milk, yeast mixture and 1¼ cups flour. Beat until smooth, about 30 seconds.
3. Gradually mix in remaining 1 cup flour and knead until smooth and elastic, about 5 minutes.
4. Form into a ball and place in greased bowl. Cover with clean kitchen cloth and let rise until double, about 1 hour.
5. Grease 9" round baking pan.
6. Divide dough into 12 pieces.
7. Lightly flour hands as needed and roll each piece in your hands, tucking ends under to make a smooth top. (This takes some practice - the rolls will still taste good even if they don't look perfect.)
8. Place rolls in prepared pan. Cover and let rise until double, at least 1 hour. Preheat oven to 375 degrees.
9. Bake 12 to 15 minutes or until golden brown.

Makes 1 dozen

FRENCH BREAD

¼ cup warm water
1 tablespoon yeast
1 cup hot water
1½ tablespoons sugar

½ tablespoon salt
¼ cup oil
3 cups flour
1 egg white

1. In small bowl, stir yeast into warm water. Let stand until yeast is dissolved, about 5 minutes.
2. In mixer bowl, combine hot water, sugar, salt and oil. Let stand to lukewarm.
3. Add dissolved yeast and 1½ cups of the flour. Beat until smooth. Add remaining flour to make soft dough that can be stirred down with a spoon.
4. Place in greased bowl and cover with clean kitchen cloth. With spoon, stir down every 10 minutes for a total of five times.
5. Turn out onto lightly floured board. Knead only enough to lightly coat with flour. Grease 2 cookie sheets.
6. Divide dough in half. Roll each into a rectangle. On long side, roll (jelly roll style) into a loaf, pinching seam with wet fingers to seal. Place each loaf, seam side down, in center of cookie sheet.
7. Beat egg white until foamy. With pastry brush, apply to loaves. Slash each loaf three times diagonally with a serrated knife. Do not cover. Let rise ½ hour.
8. Preheat oven to 400 degrees. Bake, one loaf at a time, 12 minutes or until deep golden brown. Cool completely before slicing.

Makes 2 loaves

Breadsticks:
1. Prepare French Bread dough through Step #4. Divide in half and roll each half into rectangle ½" thick on a lightly floured board.
2. With pizza cutter, cut into ¾" strips.
3. Dip each strip in melted butter and, holding both ends, turn in opposite directions several times to make a twisted rope.
4. Place on ungreased baking sheets, 2" apart.
5. Sprinkle with sesame seeds, parmesan cheese, garlic salt or favorite topping. Let rise ½ hour. Preheat oven 400 degrees.
6. Bake approximately 8 minutes or until lightly browned.

Makes 2 dozen breadsticks

FRUIT NUT LOAF

1½ cups walnuts, coarsely chopped*
1½ cups pecans, coarsely chopped*
1 cup dates, coarsely chopped
1 cup maraschino cherries,** cut in half
¾ cup flour

¾ cup sugar
½ teaspoon baking powder
½ teaspoon salt
3 eggs, beaten
1 teaspoon vanilla extract

1. Preheat oven to 325 degrees. Grease and flour 1 (9"x 5") loaf pan or 8 miniature (3½"x 2½") pans.
2. Combine nuts, dates and cherries in large mixing bowl.
3. In another bowl, stir together flour, sugar, baking powder and salt.
4. Add to nut mixture, stirring until nuts and fruits are well coated.
5. Fold eggs and vanilla into mixture and stir until all ingredients are moistened. Gently spoon into prepared pan.
6. Bake 1 hour for large loaf or 25 to 35 minutes for miniature loaves or until dry and lightly browned.
7. Cool 10 minutes in pan. Loosen edges and turn onto wire rack.

Makes 1 (9"x 5") loaf
or
12 miniature (3½"x 2½") loaves

*Substitute any variety of favorite nuts.
** Substitute raisins, dried cherries or dried cranberries.

POPPY SEED BREAD

3 cups flour
1½ teaspoons salt
1½ teaspoons baking powder
1½ cups oil
1½ teaspoons vanilla extract
1½ teaspoons almond extract
2 cups sugar

¾ cup sour cream
3 eggs
¾ cup milk
½ teaspoon butter flavoring
1½ teaspoons poppy seeds
Glaze

1. Preheat oven to 350 degrees. Grease and flour 2 (9"x 5") loaf pans or 16 miniature (3½"x 2½") pans.
2. In a bowl, combine flour, salt and baking powder. Set aside.
3. In a large mixing bowl, mix oil, vanilla, almond and sugar. Stir in sour cream. Mix well.
4. Add eggs, stirring until blended. Mix in milk, butter flavoring and poppy seeds.
5. Gradually stir in flour mixture until well blended. Spoon into prepared pans.
6. Bake large loaves approximately 1 hour and miniature loaves 20 minutes or until set in center and lightly browned on edges.
7. Cool in pan 5 minutes. Loosen edges and poke holes in top of bread with a fork.
8. Remove from pan and place on cooling rack set over large cookie sheet. Spoon glaze over warm bread.

Makes 2 (9"x 5") loaves or 16 miniature loaves

Glaze:
½ cup sugar
¼ cup orange juice
1 teaspoon vanilla extract
1 teaspoon almond extract
1 teaspoon butter flavoring

Mix together and spread over warm bread.

POTATO ROLLS

1 tablespoon yeast	1½ teaspoons salt
¼ cup warm water	2 eggs
1½ cups warm water	1 cup mashed potatoes,
⅔ cup sugar	room temperature*
⅔ cup oil	7 to 7½ cups flour

1. In a small bowl, stir yeast into ¼ cup warm water. Let sit until dissolved, about 5 minutes.
2. In large mixer bowl, using paddle attachment, combine 1½ cups warm water, sugar, oil, salt, eggs, potatoes and dissolved yeast. (Mix dough by hand if large mixer is not available.)
3. Add flour, one cup at a time to form soft dough. Place in greased bowl, cover with clean kitchen cloth and let rise until double, about 1 hour.
4. Punch down. Divide dough into three parts. Let sit 5 minutes.
5. On lightly floured board, roll each third into approximately 12" circle. With a pizza cutter, cut into 12 triangles.
6. Starting at wide end, roll each triangle into a crescent shape. Place rolls on greased baking sheet. Cover and let rise until double, about 1 hour.
7. Preheat oven to 375 degrees. Bake one pan at a time 10 minutes or until light brown.

Makes 3 dozen rolls

Use prepared instant potatoes or cooked, mashed potatoes.

Serve with butter, honey, strawberry butter or favorite spread.

Strawberry Butter:
1 (10 ounce) carton frozen strawberries, thawed and drained
1 cup butter, softened
½ cup powdered sugar

1. Combine all ingredients in food processor.
2. Blend until very smooth and lighter in color, about 10 minutes.

PUMPKIN CHOCOLATE CHIP BREAD

3 eggs, well beaten
1½ cups sugar
1¼ cups canned pumpkin
1 cup oil
2¼ cups flour
¾ teaspoon salt
¾ teaspoon baking soda

2¼ teaspoons cinnamon
¾ teaspoon nutmeg
¾ teaspoon ginger
1 cup semi-sweet chocolate chips
½ cup chopped pecans, optional

1. Preheat oven to 350 degrees.
2. Grease and flour 2 (9"x 5") loaf pans or 12 (3½"x 2½") miniature pans.
3. In large mixing bowl, blend eggs and sugar.
4. Add pumpkin and oil, mixing slightly.
5. In another bowl, combine flour, salt, baking soda, cinnamon, nutmeg and ginger.
6. Gradually add flour mixture to sugar mixture. Mix thoroughly.
7. Fold in chips and nuts, if desired.
8. Pour into prepared loaf pans and bake large loaves 50 to 60 minutes or miniature loaves approximately 22 minutes.

Makes 2 (9"x 5") loaves or 12 miniature loaves

PUMPKIN CHOCOLATE CHIP MUFFINS

1. Preheat oven to 350 degrees. Grease muffin pans or line with baking papers.
2. Mix batter for Pumpkin Chocolate Chip Bread.
3. Fill muffin pans ⅔ to ¾ full.
4. Bake approximately 25 minutes. Remove from pans and place on cooling rack.

Makes 24 muffins

QUICK BANANA BREAD

¼ - ½ cup butter, melted
3 over ripe bananas
1 cup sugar
2 eggs

1½ cups flour
½ teaspoon salt
1 teaspoon baking soda
1 cup chopped nuts, optional

1. Preheat oven to 325 degrees. Grease and flour 1 (9" x 5") loaf pan or 10 miniature (3½"x 2½") pans.
2. Melt butter and set aside to cool.
3. In mixing bowl, mash bananas well. Beat in sugar and eggs.
4. Combine flour, salt and soda. Add gradually to sugar mixture.
5. Pour in melted butter and mix well. Stir in nuts, if desired.
6. Pour into prepared loaf pans. Bake 55 to 60 minutes for large loaf or 30 minutes for miniature loaves, or until well-browned and center is set.

Makes 1 (9" x 5") loaf
or
10 (3½"x 2½") loaves

"Whoever lives true life, will love true love."
~Elizabeth Barrett Browning

SCONES

1. Make 1 recipe French Bread dough, page 57. Follow instructions 1 through 4.
2. Divide dough into fourths.
3. Roll each into 8"x 8" square.
4. With pizza cutter, cut each square into fourths.
5. Deep fry in hot oil (375 degrees) until golden brown.
6. Serve with choice of butter.

Makes 16 scones

Honey Butter:
½ cup butter, softened
¼ cup honey

1. Combine and beat until smooth.
2. If stronger honey flavor is desired, add additional honey.

Cinnamon Honey Butter:
1. Mix Honey Butter.
2. Add ⅛ teaspoon cinnamon and ⅛ teaspoon vanilla extract.

Orange Honey Butter:
1. Mix Honey Butter.
2. Add 2 teaspoons orange juice and 1 tablespoon grated orange rind.

Raspberry Butter:
½ cup butter, softened
3 tablespoons raspberry jam
3 tablespoons honey
¼ teaspoon vanilla extract

Combine and beat until smooth.

Refrigerate butters. Before serving, remove from refrigerator and let sit to room temperature or until spreadable.

WHEAT BREAD

1 tablespoon yeast
1 teaspoon sugar
¼ cup warm water
1 egg, beaten
¼ cup sugar or honey
¼ cup brown sugar

¼ cup cooking oil
1½ cups warm water
2 cups whole wheat flour
2 teaspoons salt
3 cups white flour

1. In mixer bowl, stir yeast and 1 teaspoon sugar into ¼ cup warm water. Let stand until dissolved, about 5 minutes.
2. Stir in egg, sugar, brown sugar, oil and 1½ cups warm water.
3. Add whole wheat flour and salt. Mix well and add white flour, 1 cup at a time.
4. Knead about 10 minutes until smooth and elastic.
5. Place in greased bowl and cover with clean kitchen cloth. Let rise until double, about 1 hour.
6. Grease 2 (9"x 5") loaf pans. Gently punch down dough, divide in half. Shape into 2 loaves.*
7. Place in prepared pans. Cover and let rise until double, about 1 hour.
8. Preheat oven to 350 degrees. Bake 30 minutes or until golden brown and sounds hollow when tapped.

Makes 2 (9"x 5") loaves

*To shape loaves:
On lightly floured surface, pat dough into 6"x 8" rectangle.
On long side of dough, roll up (jelly roll style).
Seal seam and place in pans, seam side down.

WHITE BREAD

1 tablespoon yeast
1 tablespoon sugar
½ cup warm water
1 egg, beaten
½ cup oil or melted shortening

2 cups lukewarm water
2 teaspoons salt
½ cup sugar
8 cups flour

1. In mixer bowl, stir yeast and 1 tablespoon sugar into ½ cup warm water. Let stand until dissolved, about 5 minutes.
2. Stir in egg, oil, water, salt and sugar.
3. Stir in flour, 1 cup at a time. Knead about 10 minutes until smooth and elastic. Place in greased bowl and cover with clean kitchen cloth. Let rise to double, approximately 1 hour.
4. Grease 3 (9"x 5") loaf pans.
5. Press down dough, just until deflated, and divide into three parts. Form into loaves.* Place in prepared pans, cover and let rise until double, about 1 hour.
6. Preheat oven to 350 degrees. Place loaves in oven several inches apart on center rack. Bake bread approximately 30 minutes. If done, loaves will be golden brown and will sound hollow when tapped.
7. Remove from oven. Loosen edges and turn onto wire rack to cool. While hot, brush tops with butter if softer crust is desired.

Makes 3 (9"x 5") loaves

To shape loaves:
On lightly floured surface, pat dough into 6"x 8" rectangle.
On long side of dough, roll up (jelly roll style).
Seal seam and place in pans, seam side down.

To make eight small loaves:
1. Follow instructions above for mixing dough.
2. Divide dough into eight pieces.
3. Shape each into a loaf and place in 8 (5½"x 3") loaf pans.
4. Preheat oven to 350 degrees. Bake approximately 15 minutes or until golden brown and loaves sound hollow when tapped.

Breakfast

Biscuits and Gravy

Blueberry Muffins

Bread Pudding

Breakfast Tortillas

Cinnamon Swirl Bread
& French Toast

Crepes

Hash Browns

Homemade Doughnuts

Homemade Syrups

Overnight Breakfast
Casserole

Pancakes

Puff Pancake

Spinach with Eggs

Veggie Omelet

Waffles

BISCUITS AND GRAVY

1 egg, well beaten
1 cup sour cream
1 tablespoon sugar
¼ cup shortening
1½ cups flour

1 teaspoon baking powder
½ teaspoon baking soda
¾ teaspoon salt
Gravy

1. Preheat oven to 400 degrees. Grease 8"x 8" baking pan.
2. In a mixing bowl, beat egg with a fork. Mix in sour cream, sugar and shortening. It is normal for small chunks of shortening to remain.
3. In another bowl, combine flour, baking powder, baking soda and salt. Add gradually to egg mixture. Mix well. Dough will be sticky.
4. Sprinkle a little flour over dough and scoop onto a well floured board. Handle dough gently.
5. Flour hands and quickly knead dough 4 strokes to form into a ball. Place smooth side up and sprinkle top lightly with flour.
6. Roll gently ¾" to 1" thickness. Cut with 2½" biscuit cutter, dipping in flour with each cut. Place in prepared pan.
7. Bake 15 minutes or until biscuits are golden brown.
8. Serve hot with gravy.

Makes 8 biscuits

Buttermilk biscuits: Substitute buttermilk for sour cream and increase flour to 2 cups.

Sausage Gravy:

¼ pound bulk sausage
3 tablespoons flour
1 cup water

1 cup milk
½ teaspoon salt
¼ teaspoon black pepper

1. Fry sausage until browned and done. Do not drain.
2. Add flour and mix into meat.
3. Add water, milk, salt and pepper.
4. Cook on medium heat 3 minutes until bubbly and thickened.

Serves 4

BLUEBERRY MUFFINS

2 cups frozen blueberries
¼ cup flour
½ cup butter, softened
1 cup sugar
2 large eggs
2 teaspoons vanilla extract

2 cups flour
2 teaspoons baking powder
¼ teaspoon salt
¼ teaspoon cinnamon
½ cup milk
Topping, optional

1. Preheat oven to 375 degrees. Line 12 standard size muffin cups with paper liners or grease muffin pan.
2. Place blueberries in colander. Rinse well and let drain. Sprinkle with ¼ cup flour. Toss gently until berries are coated with flour. Set aside.
3. In mixer bowl, cream butter and sugar.
4. Add eggs, one at a time, beating after each addition. Stir in vanilla.
5. In another bowl, combine flour, baking powder, salt and cinnamon. Gradually add to butter mixture. Mix until blended.
6. Add milk and mix lightly. Do not beat.
7. Carefully fold in blueberries. Fill muffin cups approximately ¾ full.
8. Sprinkle with Topping. Bake 25 minutes or until set and lightly browned.

Makes 12 muffins

Leftover muffins can be placed in freezer bag and frozen for later use. To reheat thawed muffins, place under broiler 30 to 60 seconds. Watch closely.

Topping:
½ cup brown sugar
2 tablespoons flour
¾ cup quick oats
¼ cup butter

1. Combine brown sugar, flour and oats.
2. With pastry blender, cut in butter until crumbly.
3. Sprinkle over muffins before baking.

BREAD PUDDING

1¼ cups warm milk
2½ cups bread cubes*
¼ cup sugar
½ teaspoon nutmeg
½ teaspoon cinnamon

½ teaspoon vanilla extract
½ cup raisins, optional
2 large eggs, slightly beaten
Sauce

1. Preheat oven to 375 degrees. Grease 9"x 5" loaf pan.
2. Combine warm milk and bread cubes in prepared pan.
3. In a mixing bowl, combine sugar, nutmeg, cinnamon and vanilla. Add raisins. Stir in eggs until well blended.
4. Pour egg mixture over bread mixture in pan and toss lightly with fork.
5. Bake until firm and puffed, about 30 minutes.
6. Remove from oven and let sit for 10 minutes. (It is normal for the bread pudding to collapse as it cools.)
7. Serve warm with sauce.

Serves 4

*Homemade bread is best, especially leftover dinner rolls.

Sauce:

¼ cup sugar
¼ cup brown sugar
¼ cup butter
¼ cup evaporated milk

1. Combine all ingredients in saucepan.
2. Heat until sugar and butter are melted. Stir often.
3. Pour over bread pudding while still hot.

BREAKFAST TORTILLAS

½ teaspoon butter
2 eggs, scrambled
1 (10") flour tortilla
2 tablespoons Cheddar cheese, grated
3 thin slices ham

1. In brunch pan or 8" skillet, melt butter.
2. Add scrambled eggs and cook, without stirring, to form an egg pancake. When set, flip and cook briefly on other side.
3. Warm tortilla in microwave for a few seconds.
4. Place egg pancake on tortilla. Sprinkle grated cheese on egg.
5. Heat ham in brunch pan and place on cheese.
6. Fold bottom half of tortilla over filling. Fold in each side and roll into a closed cylinder. Cut in half diagonally.

Makes 1 tortilla wrap

Variations:
- Fill tortilla with taco-seasoned cooked ground beef, egg pancake and cheese.
- Fill tortilla with cooked sausage, egg pancake and cheese.

CINNAMON SWIRL BREAD

1 cup milk
¼ cup butter, softened
¼ cup sugar
1 teaspoon salt
1 tablespoon dry yeast
¼ cup lukewarm water

4½ cups flour
2 eggs
2 tablespoons melted butter
3 tablespoons sugar
1 tablespoon cinnamon

1. Combine milk, butter, ¼ cup sugar and salt in mixing bowl.
2. In a small bowl, stir yeast into warm water. Let stand until dissolved, about 5 minutes. Add to milk mixture.
3. Add 2¼ cups flour and beat well. Blend in eggs. Add enough remaining flour to make soft dough. Knead about 10 minutes.
4. Place dough in greased bowl. Cover with clean kitchen cloth and let rise 1 hour or until almost double.
5. Grease 2 (9" x 5") loaf pans.
6. Divide dough in half. Roll each half in ¼" thick rectangle. Brush with melted butter. Mix cinnamon and 3 tablespoons sugar. Sprinkle over butter.
7. Roll, jelly roll style, starting at narrow end. Pinch and seal seams well with wet fingers. (If seams are not tightly sealed, bread will bulge on side and filling will escape.)
8. Place loaves seam side down in prepared pans. Cover and let rise double, about 1 hour.
9. Preheat oven to 350 degrees. Bake loaves 30 minutes. Drizzle or spread glaze over warm bread.

Makes 2 (9" x 5") loaves

Glaze:
1 cup powdered sugar
4 teaspoons milk
½ teaspoon vanilla

Combine all and drizzle over bread.

CINNAMON FRENCH TOAST
1. Omit glaze.
2. Slice Cinnamon Swirl Bread into ¾" slices.
3. Soak in beaten eggs (1 egg per 2 slices French Toast).
4. On lightly greased griddle, fry each slice until golden brown.
5. Serve hot with butter and syrup.

CREPES

1 cup flour
2 eggs
1 cup milk
½ teaspoon salt
2 tablespoons butter, melted

1. Combine all ingredients in blender in order given. Blend 1 minute, stirring down sides as needed, (or combine ingredients with a mixer or in a bowl using a whisk).
2. Use batter immediately or let set 1 hour for more tender crepes.
3. Cook in a crepe maker (following instructions) or 6" frying pan which has been greased with oil or butter.* Place about ¼ cup batter in pan and roll slightly to cover bottom of pan. When set, turn and briefly heat other side of crepe. Drop onto plate — crepes may be stacked.
4. Fill as desired. Unfilled crepes can be kept several days in refrigerator or in freezer several weeks.

Makes 12 crepes

*Caution: butter burns easily.

Suggested fillings:
- Strawberries or other fresh fruit and whipped cream.
- Breakfast filling such as scrambled egg, bacon, sausage or grated cheese.

HASH BROWNS

2 small potatoes   Cooking oil

1. Peel and grate potatoes (julienne-type grater is fun).*
2. Heat a well-oiled skillet or griddle to medium high.
3. Place a circle of grated potatoes on griddle and fry until golden brown. Turn and fry until potatoes are crisp. Add more oil as needed for desired crispness.

Serves 2

*Use diced potatoes or substitute 2 cups frozen potatoes.

For added flavor, add 2 tablespoons diced onion before frying.

"In union there is strength."

~ Aesop

HOMEMADE DOUGHNUTS

1 tablespoon yeast	½ teaspoon salt
1 tablespoon sugar	¼ cup shortening
¼ cup warm water	1 cup hot tap water
2 eggs, beaten	3½ cups flour
¼ cup sugar	Glaze

1. In small bowl, sprinkle yeast and 1 tablespoon sugar over ¼ cup warm water. Let sit until dissolved, about 5 minutes.
2. In mixing bowl, combine eggs, sugar, salt, shortening and hot tap water. Cool to lukewarm.
3. Add yeast mixture and 2 cups flour. Beat 1 minute. Gradually add remaining 1½ cups flour and mix well. Dough will be sticky. Flour hand and scoop dough into greased bowl. Form gently into a ball. Cover with clean kitchen cloth and let rise until double, about 1 hour. Punch down gently.
4. Place dough on floured board. Sprinkle top lightly with flour and gently roll or pat ½" thick. Cut with doughnut cutter (dip in flour with each cut).
5. Place doughnuts on greased cookie sheets. Cover and let rise until very light, about 1 hour.
6. In fryer or heavy saucepan, heat oil to 350 degrees. Dip turner in hot oil and slide under each doughnut. Carefully place in oil and fry each side until brown. Drain on paper towels.
7. While still hot, dip in glaze and set on rack on absorbent paper. Allow to stand until glaze is dry.

Makes 1 dozen

Glaze:
2 cups powdered sugar
⅓ cup milk
1 teaspoon vanilla extract

Combine ingredients and mix until smooth. Dip each side of doughnuts until well coated.

Chocolate Glaze:
½ cup butter
¼ cup whole milk
1 tablespoon light corn syrup

Maple Glaze:
1 cup powdered sugar
⅓ cup maple syrup
½ teaspoon maple flavoring
¼ teaspoon vanilla flavoring
2 teaspoons soft butter

Mix until smooth. Keep warm.

2 teaspoons vanilla extract
1 cup chocolate chips
1½ cups powdered sugar, sifted

1. In saucepan, combine butter, milk, corn syrup and vanilla. Heat to melt butter. Add chocolate chips and whisk until melted.
2. Turn off heat and add powdered sugar. Whisk until smooth. Keep warm.
3. Dip top of warm doughnuts in glaze and let set before serving.

HOMEMADE MAPLE SYRUP

2 cups sugar
1 cup water
1 teaspoon maple flavoring
   (or more, according to taste)

1. Mix sugar and water in saucepan. Bring to a boil.
2. Remove from heat. Add flavoring and serve hot. Syrup will be thin. (If thicker syrup is desired, boil 2 minutes.)

Makes 2 cups

HOMEMADE SYRUP

1 cup water   1 cup brown sugar
1 cup sugar   1 cup light corn syrup

1. Combine all ingredients in saucepan.
2. Bring to a full boil and boil 1 minute.

Makes 3 cups

*Syrup is extremely hot — handle carefully.
Cool at least 10 minutes before pouring.*

OVERNIGHT BREAKFAST CASSEROLE

4 slices bread, broken in pieces
1 cup cheddar cheese, grated
½ cup cooked bacon, sausage or ham pieces
3 eggs, beaten
1 cup milk
¼ teaspoon dry mustard, optional
1 (10 ¾ ounce) can cream of mushroom soup
½ cup milk
½ cup Cheddar cheese, shredded

1. Place bread in bottom of greased 8"x 8" baking pan.
2. Sprinkle 1 cup cheese over top.
3. Break cooked meat into pieces and scatter over cheese.
4. In mixing bowl, beat eggs, 1 cup milk and dry mustard. Pour over bread mixture.
5. Cover and refrigerate overnight.
6. In the morning, preheat oven to 300 degrees.
7. Mix soup and ½ cup milk to make about 2 cups.
8. Spoon 1 cup soup mixture over casserole. (Store remaining topping in refrigerator in airtight container for up to 10 days.)
9. Bake uncovered for one hour. Sprinkle ½ cup cheese last 10 minutes baking time.

Serves 4

PANCAKES

1 cup flour
1 teaspoon baking powder
½ teaspoon salt
1 tablespoon sugar

1 cup milk*
1 egg, lightly beaten
¼ cup oil or melted butter

1. In mixing bowl, combine flour, baking powder, salt and sugar.
2. In another bowl, mix milk, egg and oil. Add to flour mixture and stir just until blended. (It is normal for some small lumps to remain in batter. Batter should be slightly thick but pourable. Add an additional tablespoon milk, if needed.)
3. Preheat griddle or skillet to medium-high and brush with oil.
4. With ladle, pour approximately ¼ cup batter onto hot griddle for each pancake.
5. Flip pancake over when bubbles form and edges are set. Flip only once and do not flatten pancake while cooking.
6. Cook until golden brown. Serve with homemade syrup.

Makes 6 (5") pancakes

*For lighter pancakes, use 3/4 cup milk and ½ cup sour cream.

Wheat pancakes:
Use ½ cup whole wheat flour and ½ cup white flour.

Buttermilk pancakes:
1. Substitute buttermilk for milk.
2. Add ¼ teaspoon baking soda to dry ingredients.

PUFF PANCAKE

¼ cup butter
6 eggs
1 cup milk
1 cup flour

⅛ teaspoon salt
fresh fruit of choice
whipped cream

1. Preheat oven to 400 degrees.
2. Place butter in 9"x 13" pan and heat in oven until melted.
3. Whip eggs, milk, flour and salt in blender or with mixer. Pour into prepared pan.
4. Bake uncovered approximately 20 minutes or until puffed and golden brown.
5. Top with fresh fruit and whipped cream.

Serves 6

For fancy brunch, prepare in 8"round casserole dish. Reduce ingredients to:

3 tablespoons butter
4 eggs
¾ cup milk

¾ cup flour
⅛ teaspoon salt

1. Preheat oven to 400 degrees.
2. Place butter in casserole dish and heat in oven until melted.
3. Whip eggs, milk, flour and salt in blender or with mixer. Pour into prepared pan.
4. Bake uncovered approximately 20 minutes or until puffed and golden brown (When you remove from oven, the pancake will collapse, forming a bowl shape.)
5. Fill with fresh peaches, strawberries, kiwi or other favorite fruits.
6. Top with whipped cream.

Serves 4

SPINACH WITH EGGS

1 teaspoon butter, divided
2 ounces fresh baby spinach
¼ teaspoon salt
⅛ teaspoon pepper
3 eggs
1 tablespoon cheese, grated

1. Melt ½ teaspoon butter in skillet. Add spinach and stir fry until wilted.
2. Sprinkle with salt and pepper. Remove spinach from pan.
3. Empty excess moisture from skillet and wipe it out. Melt ½ teaspoon butter in pan.
4. Beat eggs and scramble in pan until almost done, but not dry.
5. Continue cooking eggs while stirring in spinach.
6. Spoon mixture into small casserole and sprinkle top with grated cheese. Serve immediately.

Serves 2

"'Once upon a time' is a nice beginning, but it takes two to create 'happily ever after.'"
~Celia Jolley

VEGGIE OMELET

3 eggs, well beaten
1 tablespoon cooking oil
½ cup veggies of choice*
¼ cup cheese, shredded

1. Heat oil in 8" skillet over medium heat. Add eggs and cook until set. (Or use omelet pan and follow instructions for use.)
2. Sprinkle veggies and cheese over omelet.
3. With egg turner, lift one side of omelet and fold over.
4. Top with chopped veggies and shredded cheese, if desired.

Makes 1 large omelet

*chopped tomatoes, diced bell pepper, sliced mushrooms, chopped or sliced sautéed onion, or sliced avocado

WAFFLES

1 cup flour
1½ teaspoons baking powder
¼ teaspoon salt
2 teaspoons sugar

1 egg
1 cup milk
¼ cup oil

1. Preheat waffle iron.
2. In a bowl, combine flour, baking powder, salt and sugar.
3. In another bowl, mix egg, milk and oil. Add flour mixture and stir just until moistened. (It is normal for some small lumps to remain in batter.)
4. Bake according to waffle iron instructions.
5. Serve with favorite topping.

Serves 4

Suggested Toppings:
Brown Sugar Topping
Butter & syrup
Peanut butter & syrup
Strawberries (or other favorite fruits) & whipped cream

Brown Sugar Topping:
2 tablespoons brown sugar
¼ cup sour cream (can use non-fat or light)
Strawberries

1. Combine brown sugar and sour cream. Mix well.
2. Spread on waffles and top with strawberries.

Cakes & desserts

Apple Harvest Cake

Cherry Chocolate Cake

Chocolate Cake

Cream Cheese Carrot Cake

Family Favorite Cake

Lemon Cake

Oatmeal Cake with Frosting

Sour Cream Cake

White Wedding Cake

White Wedding Cake Frosting

White Wedding Fondant
& Chocolate Fondant

. . . .

Apple Crisp &
Apple Caramel Sundaes

Apple Pie

Baked Meringue
with Peaches & Cream

Banana Pudding

Berry Cobbler

Cheesecake

Chocolate Dessert

Fruit Parfait

Ice Cream Pie

Key Lime Pie

Trifle

APPLE HARVEST CAKE

2 cups sugar
½ cup butter, softened
2 eggs, beaten
2 cups flour
2 teaspoons baking soda

2 teaspoons cinnamon
½ teaspoon nutmeg
1 teaspoon salt
4 cups peeled, shredded apples
1 cup chopped nuts, optional

1. Preheat oven to 350 degrees. Grease and flour 9"x 13" pan.
2. In mixing bowl, cream sugar and butter until well blended. Stir in eggs.
3. In another bowl, combine flour, baking soda, cinnamon, nutmeg and salt. Add to creamed mixture and mix well.
4. Stir in nuts and apples. Spread in prepared pan.
5. Bake 35 minutes.
6. Top with desired sauce and whipped cream.

Serves 15

Caramel sauce:
½ cup sugar
½ cup brown sugar
½ cup evaporated milk
½ cup butter
1 teaspoon flour
1 teaspoon vanilla

1. Combine sugar, brown sugar, milk, butter and flour in saucepan. Heat until butter is melted.
2. Bring to a boil and gently boil until sugar is dissolved, about 2 minutes. Add vanilla.

Butter sauce:
¾ cup butter
1½ cups sugar
¾ cup evaporated milk
½ teaspoon vanilla extract

1. Melt butter over low heat. Add sugar and milk.
2. Stir until mixture is creamy.
3. Remove from heat and add vanilla.

CHERRY CHOCOLATE CAKE

1 devil's food moist cake mix
½ cup water, optional
3 eggs, beaten
1 teaspoon almond extract
1 (21 ounce) can cherry pie filling
Fudge Frosting

1. Preheat oven to 350 degrees. Grease and flour 9"x 13" pan.
2. In mixer bowl, combine cake mix, water, eggs and almond extract.
3. Beat 2 minutes on medium speed.
4. With large spoon, gently fold in pie filling until well blended.
5. Pour batter into prepared pan and bake 40 minutes.
6. Frost warm cake.

Serves 15

Fudge Frosting:
1 cup sugar
5 tablespoons butter
⅓ cup whole milk
1 cup semi-sweet chocolate chips

1. Mix sugar, butter and milk in a saucepan and bring to a boil.
2. Boil 1 minute, stirring constantly.
3. Turn off heat and stir in chocolate chips until melted and smooth.
4. Let cool until warm before pouring onto cake.

CHOCOLATE CAKE

2¼ cups flour
2 cups sugar
¾ cup baking cocoa
1½ teaspoons baking powder
1½ teaspoons baking soda
½ teaspoon salt

1¾ cups water
¾ cup milk
¾ cup oil
3 eggs
2 teaspoons vanilla extract
Frosting

1. Preheat oven to 350 degrees.
2. Grease and flour 2 (9") round pans or 1 (9"x 13") pan.*
3. In mixer bowl, combine flour, sugar, cocoa, baking powder, baking soda and salt. Mix until well blended.
4. Add water, milk, oil, eggs and vanilla. Beat 2 minutes on medium speed.
5. Pour batter into prepared pan and bake 35 minutes or until tooth pick comes out clean. Cool 10 minutes in pan.
6. Spray cooling rack with cooking spray. Turn cake onto rack. Cool completely. Frost.

Serves 15

For cream cake, grease and flour 3 or 4 (9") round cake pans. Divide batter evenly between pans and bake 15 minutes. Cool and fill layers with whipped cream. Frost with Chocolate frosting or Magic frosting.

Chocolate Buttercream Frosting:

½ cup baking cocoa
3 cups powdered sugar
½ cup butter, softened

1/3 cup milk
1 teaspoon vanilla extract

1. In mixer bowl, combine cocoa and powdered sugar.
2. Add soft butter, milk and vanilla. Beat until smooth and creamy.

Makes 2 cups

CREAM CHEESE CARROT CAKE

2 cups sugar
4 eggs
1½ cups oil
1 teaspoon vanilla extract
3 cups grated carrot
   (about 4 large carrots)

1 (8 ounce) package cream
   cheese, softened
2 cups flour
1 teaspoon salt
2 teaspoons baking soda
1 teaspoon cinnamon

1. Preheat oven to 350 degrees. Grease and flour 9"x 13" baking pan.
2. In large mixing bowl, mix sugar, eggs, oil and vanilla.
3. Stir in carrots and cream cheese until well blended.
4. In another bowl, combine dry ingredients and add to sugar mixture.
5. Spread in prepared pan.
6. Bake 55 minutes. Cool and frost.

Serves 24

Variation: Add 1 cup raisins and 1 cup chopped nuts.

Cream Cheese Frosting:

¼ cup butter, softened
1 (8 ounce) package cream
   cheese, softened
1 pound powdered sugar
   (about 3 ¾ cups)

2 tablespoons milk
1 teaspoon vanilla extract

Combine and spread on cooled cake.

FAMILY FAVORITE CAKE

1. Prepare any flavor cake mix according to package directions (chocolate or strawberry are especially good).
2. Divide batter between 4 (9") greased round cake pans.
3. Bake 15 minutes or until cake tests done. Cool 10 minutes in pan.
4. Turn onto cooling racks and cool completely.
5. Frost layers with whipped cream and stack.
6. Frost top and sides with Magic Frosting.

Serves 15

Magic Frosting:
2 egg whites
1 cup sugar
¼ teaspoon salt
¼ teaspoon cream of tartar
5 tablespoons cold water
1 teaspoon vanilla extract

1. Place egg whites in mixer bowl.
2. In small saucepan, mix sugar, salt, cream of tartar and cold water. Bring to a full boil over medium heat.
3. Slowly pour boiled mixture over egg whites while beating at medium speed. Add vanilla.
4. Beat high speed until stiff peaks form.

Frosts 9" layer cake or 9"x 13" cake.

Tip: Pasteurized eggs are recommended for Magic Frosting.

LEMON CAKE

1 Lemon Cake Mix
1 (3 ounce) package lemon gelatin
4 eggs
1¼ cups water
½ cup cooking oil
Lemon Glaze

1. Preheat oven to 350 degrees.
2. Grease and flour 9"x 13" cake pan or 10" Bundt pan.
3. In mixer bowl, combine cake mix, gelatin, eggs, water and oil. Beat two minutes on medium speed.
4. Pour into prepared baking pan.
5. Bake 30 to 35 minutes for 9"x 13" pan or 45 to 50 minutes for Bundt pan.
6. Remove from oven and cool 10 minutes. For Bundt cake, turn onto cooling rack.
7. While cake is still hot, poke holes in cake with a fork. Spread glaze evenly over cake.
8. To serve, cut into squares or slices. Serve plain or top with whipped topping sprinkled with lemon zest.*

Serves 15

*For lemon zest, use a zester or fine grater to shave peel from a fresh lemon.

Lemon Glaze:
2 cups powdered sugar
⅓ cup lemon juice

Mix together and spread over hot cake.

OATMEAL CAKE
WITH COCONUT PECAN FROSTING

1½ cups boiling water
1 cup quick oats
½ cup oil or butter, softened
2 eggs
1 cup sugar

1 cup brown sugar
1½ cups flour
1 teaspoon baking soda
½ teaspoon salt
1 teaspoon cinnamon

1. Preheat oven to 350 degrees. Grease 9"x 13" baking pan.
2. In a metal bowl, pour boiling water over oats. Let stand while preparing batter.
3. In mixing bowl, mix oil or butter, eggs, sugar and brown sugar.
4. In another bowl, combine flour, soda, salt and cinnamon. Stir gradually into sugar mixture.
5. Add oatmeal and mix well. Spread in prepared pan.
6. Bake 30 minutes. Spread with frosting while hot.

Serves 15

Coconut Pecan Frosting:
1 cup brown sugar
½ cup evaporated milk
½ cup butter
1 teaspoon vanilla
½ cup chopped pecans*
1 cup coconut

1. In saucepan, heat brown sugar and milk until sugar is dissolved.
2. Add butter and stir almost constantly until mixture boils and becomes thick, about 3 to 5 minutes. Remove from heat.
3. Add vanilla, nuts, and coconut. Pour on cake while hot.

*Substitute other nuts, if desired.

SOUR CREAM CAKE

4 eggs, separated
2 cups sugar
1 cup oil
1 cup sour cream
1 cup buttermilk

1 teaspoon vanilla extract
2 cups flour
½ teaspoon salt
½ teaspoon baking soda
1 teaspoon baking powder

1. Preheat oven to 350 degrees.
2. Grease and flour 10" bundt pan, 9"x 13" cake pan or 2 (9") round cake pans.
3. Separate eggs and place egg whites in mixer bowl. Beat until stiff peaks form. Set aside. Reserve egg yolks.
4. In large mixing bowl, by hand (do not use mixer), mix sugar and oil. Add egg yolks, sour cream, buttermilk and vanilla.
5. In another bowl, combine flour, salt, baking soda, and baking powder. Gradually stir into sugar mixture.
6. Fold in beaten egg whites. Pour into prepared pan.
7. Bake approximately 50 minutes for bundt pan, 35 minutes for 9"x 13" or 30 minutes for 9" rounds until cake is well browned and toothpick comes out clean.
8. Use as cake for strawberry shortcake or frost with caramel frosting.

Serves 15

Caramel Frosting:
½ cup butter
1 cup brown sugar
¼ cup milk

1 teaspoon vanilla extract
2 cups powdered sugar

1. In saucepan, melt butter.
2. Add brown sugar and stir on medium low heat until sugar dissolves, about 2 minutes.
3. Add milk and remove from heat. Stir in vanilla. Cool slightly, about 2 minutes.
4. Whisk in powdered sugar until frosting is a smooth spreading consistency. Add additional powdered sugar if necessary.

WHITE WEDDING CAKE

8 egg whites
2 cups sugar
1 cup oil
1 cup sour cream
1 cup buttermilk

1 teaspoon clear vanilla extract*
2 cups flour
½ teaspoon baking soda
1 teaspoon baking powder
½ teaspoon salt

1. Preheat oven to 350 degrees. Grease and flour 2 (8") round cake pans or 1 (10" or 12") pan.
2. In mixer bowl, beat egg whites until stiff peaks form. Set aside.
3. In large mixing bowl, by hand, mix sugar and oil. (Do not use mixer.)
4. Add sour cream, buttermilk and vanilla.
5. In another bowl, combine flour, soda, baking powder and salt. Gradually add to sugar mixture.
6. Fold in beaten egg whites. Pour into prepared pans. (For 10" layer, decrease batter by 1 cup.)
7. Bake approximately 30 minutes for 8" layers, 35 minutes for larger layers, or until cake is browned and toothpick comes out clean.
8. Remove cake from oven and let cool in pan 10 minutes. Loosen edges and turn onto cooling rack.
9. When cold, frost with white wedding cake frosting. To cover with fondant, do not frost and follow directions on Fondant recipe, page 127.

Makes 2 (8") layers or 1 (10"or 12") layer

Substitute almond extract, if preferred.

For later use, wrap and freeze unfrosted cake layers.

Groom's Cake:
1. Prepare Chocolate Cake recipe, page 113 and bake in greased 9" heart shaped spring-form pan.
2. Cool and frost with very thin coat of chocolate frosting.
3. Cover with chocolate fondant and decorate as desired.

WHITE WEDDING CAKE FROSTING

4 cups powdered sugar
2/3 cup white shortening

3 tablespoons milk
1 teaspoon clear vanilla extract

1. In mixer bowl, combine all ingredients on low speed.
2. Increase mixer speed to high and beat until smooth.
3. Spread thin layer of frosting on cake.

Makes 2½ cups

To frost cake:
Place one layer on cake board or plate. Frost and then place second layer on top. Frost sides, then top of cake.

To smooth frosting:
1. Run hot water over spreader and dry well.
2. Smooth frosting using edge of spreader. Wipe frosting from spreader with paper towel each time you move to another spot.
3. After frosting, allow to sit 5 minutes.
4. Place a smooth paper towel (one with no texture) over frosted cake and smooth with clean spreader. Can smooth as much as needed; get clean paper towel if frosting begins to stick (or use wax paper).
5. Decorate as desired.

WHITE WEDDING FONDANT

2 pounds (about 7½ cups) powdered sugar
2 tablespoons water
1 (16 ounce) package mini marshmallows

1. Place half the powdered sugar in large bowl and make indentation in center.
2. Combine water and marshmallows in saucepan or double boiler and heat low until marshmallows are melted. (To melt in microwave: Place in microwave safe bowl and stir every 20 seconds until melted.)
3. Pour into center of powdered sugar and mix carefully. Add as much of remaining powdered sugar as needed, a little at a time. Knead with hands until pliable. (It can be mixed and kneaded with dough hook in large professional stand mixer.) If still sticky, add powdered sugar as needed.
4. Wrap well in plastic or place in plastic food bag and seal until ready to use. Fondant is easier to handle if allowed to sit several hours.
5. To prepare cake to be covered with fondant, mix 2 cups powdered sugar with 1 cup water to make a thick glaze. Spread with pastry brush over cake. This makes a sticky surface to hold the fondant to the cake.
6. When ready to use, if fondant is too stiff to roll easily, place in microwave a few seconds until pliable. Knead until smooth.
7. Using long rolling pin, roll fondant on table or countertop dusted with powdered sugar (or spray countertop and rolling pin with cooking spray). Do not turn fondant over. Each time you roll, shift fondant around slightly to make sure it is not sticking to table. Roll to 5 inches larger than cake you are covering. For example, to cover 8", 2 layer cake, roll fondant to 13" circle. Roll approximately ¼" thick for easy handling.
8. Lay fondant over cake and smooth with hands. If air bubbles form, prick bubble with sharp pin and smooth area. Trim edges with scissors or pizza cutter. Makes enough to cover a 2 layer (8") cake.

Chocolate Fondant:
After melting marshmallows, add 8 ounces melted semi-sweet chocolate and 5 tablespoons baking cocoa powder. Stir well. Continue with steps 3 through 8.

APPLE CRISP

3 medium apples
2 tablespoons sugar
½ teaspoon cinnamon
¾ cup rolled oats

¾ cup brown sugar
½ cup flour
½ cup butter, slightly softened

1. Preheat oven to 350 degrees. Butter 8"x 8" baking dish or 8" pie plate.
2. Wash, peel and core apples. Slice thinly and place in prepared dish.
3. Mix sugar and cinnamon. Sprinkle over apples and toss lightly.
4. In mixing bowl, combine oats, brown sugar and flour.
5. Cut in butter until mixture is crumbly. Scatter over apples.
6. Bake 35 to 40 minutes.

Serves 6

CARAMEL APPLE SUNDAES
1. Fill individual serving bowls with apple crisp.
2. Add scoop vanilla ice cream.
3. Drizzle caramel topping over all.
4. Top with toasted pecan halves and serve.

To toast pecans: Preheat oven to 350 degrees. Spread pecans in single layer on ungreased cookie sheet. Bake 5 minutes, stirring occasionally, until toasted.

APPLE PIE

Filling:
- 2/3 cup sugar
- 1/3 cup brown sugar, packed
- 1/3 cup flour
- 2 teaspoons cinnamon
- 8 large peeled, cored and sliced apples*

1. Combine sugar, brown sugar, flour and cinnamon.
2. Place apples in large mixing bowl and sprinkle with sugar mixture. Stir until apples are well coated.

Crust:
- 2½ cups flour
- 1¼ teaspoons salt
- 1 tablespoon sugar
- 1 cup shortening
- 1¼ teaspoons white vinegar
- 1 egg, beaten
- ¼ cup cold water
- 1 tablespoon butter

1. Preheat oven to 350 degrees.
2. In mixing bowl, combine flour, salt, and sugar. With pastry blender, cut in shortening until mixture is crumbly.
3. Combine vinegar, egg and cold water. Sprinkle over flour mixture, while stirring, until dough forms a ball. If needed, add 1 or 2 tablespoons more water.
4. Cut dough in half and form each half into a ball. On floured board, roll one half into 12" circle and line 9" deep pie plate with it. (If dough tears or a hole forms in it, pinch dough together to repair.) Trim to edge of pie plate.
5. Arrange filling in crust, pressing down gently to eliminate spaces. Cut 1 tablespoon butter into pieces and scatter over filling.
6. Roll second half of the dough into 12" circle and lay over top of filling. Trim dough ½" to 1" larger than pie plate. Tuck top edge under bottom crust edge. Flute edges by pinching dough together every ½" along edge.
7. Brush top with milk and sprinkle with sugar. Cut several slits in crust to vent. Bake 1 hour 15 minutes. If crust begins to brown too much on edges, cover with foil.

Makes 1 (9") deep dish pie

Combine tart apples, such as Granny Smith and mild apples, such as Gala.

BAKED MERINGUE WITH PEACHES N' CREAM

3 egg whites
¾ cup sugar
1 teaspoon cornstarch
1 teaspoon vanilla extract
1 teaspoon white vinegar

1½ tablespoons boiling water
½ pint whipping cream
¼ cup sugar
1 teaspoon vanilla extract

1. Preheat oven to 250 degrees. Generously grease and flour a large cookie sheet. Lay an 8" paper plate in center of cookie sheet. Trace around it with your finger. Remove plate.
2. Place egg whites in cold mixing bowl.* Beat until fluffy.
3. Add ¾ cup sugar slowly while continuing to beat until stiff.
4. Stir in cornstarch, 1 teaspoon vanilla, vinegar and boiling water. Beat until mixture holds its shape.
5. Pile mixture inside circle on prepared cookie sheet. Spread evenly to the edges of the circle.
6. Bake 1 hour or until surface is dry. Allow to cool about 5 minutes.
7. Using an egg turner, loosen the meringue disk from cookie sheet and allow to cool 20 minutes. Using two large egg turners, transfer the meringue to serving dish or large pie plate.
8. With mixer, beat whipping cream until thickened. Add ¼ cup sugar and beat until peaks form. Continue beating while adding 1 teaspoon vanilla.
9. Top cooled meringue with whipped cream and peaches or fresh fruit of your choice.

Serves 4

*Egg whites will not whip to full volume if any egg yolk is present.

"Happiness is being married to your best friend."

~Anonymous

BANANA PUDDING

½ (12 ounce) box vanilla wafers
3 large bananas
1 (5.1 ounce) instant vanilla pudding mix*
1½ cups whipped topping or whipped cream
¼ cup chopped nuts, optional

1. Prepare instant pudding according to pie instructions on package.
2. Layer ingredients in 1½ quart clear serving bowl as follows:

   - Vanilla wafers to cover bottom of bowl
   - Slice 1 banana over wafers
   - Spoon 1 cup pudding over bananas.
   - Continue until you have 3 layers each of wafers, bananas and pudding. Cover top with extra wafers.
   - Top with whipped topping or whipped cream and sprinkle with nuts, if desired.

3. Refrigerate until well chilled.

Serves 6

*Substitute 3 cups favorite vanilla or banana pudding.

BERRY COBBLER

1½ tablespoons butter, softened
½ cup sugar
1 cup flour
1 teaspoon baking powder
½ teaspoon salt

½ cup milk
1 cup berries*
½ cup sugar
1 cup boiling water

1. Preheat oven to 350 degrees. Spray 8" or 9" baking dish with cooking spray.
2. In mixing bowl, cream butter and ½ cup sugar.
3. In another bowl, combine flour, baking powder and salt. Add to creamed mixture.
4. Gradually stir in milk and mix until well blended.
5. Spread in prepared baking pan. Scatter berries over top of batter.
6. Sprinkle ½ cup sugar over berries. Slowly pour boiling water over all.
7. Bake 40 minutes or until golden brown. Cool 10 minutes.
8. Serve with whipped cream or vanilla ice cream.

Serves 6

*blackberries, raspberries or other favorite berries

CHEESECAKE

Crust:
>1 cup graham cracker crumbs
>¼ cup butter, melted
>2 tablespoons sugar

1. Preheat oven to 350 degrees. Butter 9" pie plate.
2. Mix all ingredients well. Press into prepared pie plate.
3. Bake 10 minutes. Set aside.

Filling:
>2 (8 ounce) packages cream cheese
>¾ cup sugar
>2 eggs
>1 cup sour cream
>1 teaspoon vanilla extract or lime juice

1. In glass mixing bowl, soften cream cheese in microwave on defrost setting for 2 minutes.
2. Add sugar and mix until well blended. A sturdy metal whisk works great.
3. Whisk in eggs, sour cream and vanilla or lime juice.
4. Pour into prepared crust and bake 25 or 30 minutes.
5. Cheesecake will be slightly jiggly. It will set as it cools.
6. Top with favorite fruit topping.

Makes 1 (9") Cheesecake

CHOCOLATE DESSERT

Layer 1: CRUST
    ½ cup flour
    ¼ cup finely chopped nuts
    ¼ cup cold butter

1. Preheat oven to 350 degrees.
2. In mixing bowl, combine flour and nuts.
3. Cut in butter with pastry blender. Press into 8" square baking dish. Bake 15 minutes. Cool completely.

Layer 2: CREAM CHEESE FILLING
    ½ pint whipping cream
    ¼ cup sugar
    ½ cup powdered sugar
    4 ounces cream cheese, softened

4. With mixer, beat cream until thickened. Add ¼ cup sugar and continue to beat until peaks form.
5. Combine powdered sugar and cream cheese. Fold in half whipped cream. (Reserve other half for Topping.)
6. Spread over crust. Refrigerate while preparing filling.

Layer 3: PIE FILLING
    1 (3.5 ounce) instant chocolate pudding mix

7. Prepare according to directions on package. Cover with plastic wrap and refrigerate until chilled.
8. Spread over cream cheese mixture.

Layer 4: TOPPING
    Whipped cream
    ¼ cup grated milk chocolate

9. Spread reserved whipped cream over pie filling and top with grated chocolate. Refrigerate until serving time.

Serves 9

FRUIT PARFAIT

2 cups mixed fruit, suggested variety:
- Peaches
- Bananas
- Pineapple
- Strawberries
- Grapes
- Apples

Lime juice
3 tablespoons yogurt, flavor of choice
Coconut macaroons

1. Divide fruit into 2 bowls or 2 parfait glasses.
2. Sprinkle with lime juice.
3. Spoon yogurt over each serving.
4. Top with crumbled coconut macaroons.

Serves 2

"If music be the food of love: play on."
~William Shakespeare

ICE CREAM PIE

⅔ cup brown sugar, packed
⅓ cup butter, softened
½ cup nuts, chopped
½ cup flaked coconut
2 cups cornflakes, crushed
1 quart ice cream, softened

1. Mix all ingredients except ice cream. Press into 9" pie plate. Chill.
2. Fill crust* with softened ice cream. Refreeze.
3. Serve with Hot Fudge Topping or Berry Topping.

Makes 1 (9") pie

*Substitute prepared graham or chocolate cookie crust, if desired.

Hot Fudge Topping:
2 cups sugar
¼ cup baking cocoa
½ cup butter
¾ cup evaporated milk
2 teaspoons vanilla extract

1. Stir and heat sugar and cocoa over low heat.
2. Add butter and stir constantly until melted.
3. Gradually add milk and bring to boil. Boil 2 minutes.
4. Remove from heat and cool slightly. Add vanilla.
5. Serve warm.

Berry Topping:
1. Prepare 1 box strawberry or raspberry Danish dessert mix according to package directions. Chill.
2. Slice 1 pint fresh strawberries and mix into chilled mixture.

KEY LIME PIE

1 (8") baked pie crust or graham cracker crust
4 egg yolks
1 (14 ounce) can sweetened condensed milk
½ cup fresh or bottled lime juice
Zest of one lime
Drop of green food coloring
Whipped cream

1. Preheat oven to 350 degrees.
2. Place egg yolks in small mixer bowl. Beat 1 minute on medium speed or until yolks are frothy and deep lemon color.
3. Continue beating on low speed and gradually add sweetened condensed milk. Beat 1 minute.
4. Continue beating while slowly adding lime juice. The mixture will thicken immediately.
5. Beat only until all ingredients are well combined and mixture is smooth. If more flavor is desired, add zest of one lime.
6. Add drop of green food coloring, if desired. Spoon filling into cooled pie crust. Bake 30 minutes, until set.
7. Cool and refrigerate. Top with whipped cream before serving.

Makes 1 (8") pie

TRIFLE

1 (3 ounce) package strawberry gelatin
1 (3.4 ounce) package instant cheesecake pudding mix*
1 (11 ounce) angel food cake loaf
2 cups strawberries
2 medium bananas
½ pint whipping cream
¼ cup sugar
1 teaspoon vanilla extract

1. Mix gelatin according to package directions. Refrigerate until slightly thickened.
2. Prepare pudding mix according to package directions. Set aside.
3. Cut angel food cake in half. Break up one half the cake and place in 3 quart trifle bowl.
4. Cap, wash and slice strawberries into halves. Sprinkle one cup berries over cake in bowl.
5. Pour one cup thickened gelatin over cake and fruit.
6. Slice one banana over mixture in bowl. Top with half the pudding.
7. Whip cream in small mixing bowl with sugar and vanilla.
8. Spread whipped cream over pudding layer.
9. Repeat layers, ending with whipped cream and garnish with extra berries, if desired.

Serves 12

*Substitute vanilla or white chocolate instant pudding mix.

Cookies

Brownies

Chocolate Chip Cookies

Christmas Wreaths

Cookie Frosting

Gingerbread Boys

Ginger Snap Cookies

Halloween Peanut Butter Fingers

Lemon Bars

Marshmallow Brownies

No-Bake Chocolate Cookies

Oatmeal Raisin Cookies

Peanut Butter Bars

Peanut Butter Cookies & Kiss Cookies

Raspberry Thumbprints

Snickerdoodles

Sugar Cookies

White Wedding Cookies

BROWNIES

1½ cups flour
½ cup baking cocoa
¼ teaspoon baking powder
½ teaspoon salt
2 cups sugar

1 cup butter, softened
4 eggs
2 teaspoons vanilla extract
2 cups chocolate chips*
1½ cups chopped nuts, optional

1. Preheat oven to 350 degrees. Grease bottom only of 9"x13" pan (or spray pan with cooking spray then line with parchment paper).
2. In mixing bowl, combine flour, cocoa, baking powder and salt. Set aside.
3. In another bowl, cream sugar, butter, eggs and vanilla. Gradually stir flour mixture into creamed mixture.
4. Stir in chocolate chips and nuts.
5. Spread in prepared pan and bake 28 to 30 minutes. Brownies are done when top is glossy and small cracks begin to form. Cool completely.
6. Sprinkle with powdered sugar or frost with chocolate frosting. Cut into squares.

Makes 2 dozen

*Butterscotch chips, peanut butter chips or mint chips can be substituted for all or part of chocolate chips.

CHOCOLATE CHIP COOKIES

1 cup butter, softened
1 cup sugar
1 cup brown sugar, packed
2 eggs
2 teaspoons vanilla extract

3 cups flour
1 teaspoon baking soda
1 teaspoon baking powder
2 cups chocolate chips*

1. Preheat oven to 350 degrees.
2. In mixing bowl, cream butter, sugar and brown sugar.
3. Add eggs and vanilla. Mix well.
4. In another bowl, combine flour, baking soda and baking powder. Add gradually to sugar mixture.
5. Fold in chocolate chips. Roll dough into 1" balls.
6. Place on ungreased cookie sheets or line with parchment paper and flatten slightly.
7. Bake 10 minutes or until tops have small cracks on surface and cookie is lightly browned. For softer cookies, do not over bake.

Makes 3 dozen

*Use 1 cup semi-sweet and 1 cup milk chocolate chips if desired.

CHRISTMAS WREATHS

32 large marshmallows
½ cup butter
1 teaspoon vanilla or almond extract
2 teaspoons green food coloring
4½ cups corn flake cereal
Red hot candies (or other small round red candies)

1. In saucepan, melt marshmallows and butter. Remove from heat.
2. Stir in extract and food coloring. Add corn flake cereal. Stir well.
3. Drop by tablespoons onto wax paper and shape into wreaths. (It helps to butter fingers slightly.)
4. Immediately press three red hot candies, spaced evenly, to decorate.
5. Leave on wax paper, uncovered, until set.

Makes 2 dozen

"Today we plant the seeds. Tomorrow we harvest the flowers."
~ Anonymous

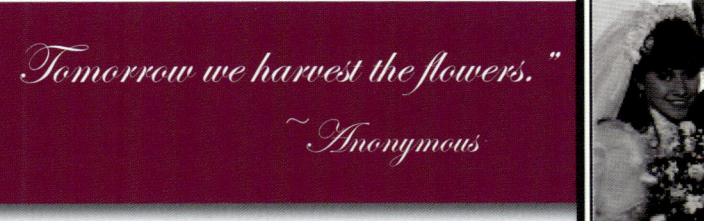

COOKIE FROSTING

Buttercream Frosting:

½ cup butter, softened
1 teaspoon vanilla extract
3 cups powdered sugar
2 tablespoons milk

1. Beat butter and vanilla with electric mixer until creamy.
2. Add powdered sugar, one cup at a time, beating after each addition.
3. Add milk and beat. Tint with food coloring, if desired.
4. Frost cooled cookies.
5. Add any sprinkles or decorations you desire immediately after frosting.

Makes 2 cups

Cookie Glaze:

2 cups powdered sugar
1 tablespoon milk
6 tablespoons light corn syrup

1. Mix powdered sugar, milk and corn syrup. Add more corn syrup, a tablespoon at a time, to thin, if needed. Tint with food coloring if desired.
2. If sprinkles or other decorations are used, add immediately after frosting.

Makes 1 cup

This is a flow frosting – it should be a fairly thick consistency but still spreadable. The frosting will flow slightly to give a smooth look.

GINGERBREAD BOYS

½ cup shortening
½ cup sugar
½ cup dark molasses
1 egg
2 ½ cups flour

½ teaspoon baking soda
1 teaspoon baking powder
1 teaspoon ginger
1 ½ teaspoons cinnamon

1. In mixing bowl, cream shortening and sugar.
2. Add molasses and beat until fluffy. Beat in egg.
3. In another bowl, combine flour, soda, baking powder, ginger and cinnamon. Gradually add to creamed mixture and mix well.
4. Cover and chill 1 hour. Preheat oven to 350 degrees. Lightly grease cookie sheet or line with parchment paper.
5. Roll dough to ¼" thickness and cut out with gingerbread boy, girl or other 3" cookie cutters.* Place 2" apart on cookie sheet.
6. Bake approximately 10 minutes until cookies are set and do not look doughy in center.
7. Let cool and decorate as desired.

Makes 1 ½ dozen

*If using a different size cookie cutter, adjust baking time.

GINGERSNAP COOKIES

2 cups flour	¾ cup shortening or butter
1 teaspoon ginger	1 cup sugar
1 teaspoon cinnamon	1 egg
1 teaspoon baking soda	¼ cup molasses
½ teaspoon salt	Sugar for rolling

1. Preheat oven to 350 degrees. Lightly grease cookie sheet or line with parchment paper.
2. In medium bowl, combine flour, ginger, cinnamon, soda and salt.
3. In mixer bowl, cream shortening and sugar. Add egg and molasses and mix well. Gradually stir in flour mixture.
4. Form into 1½" balls and roll in sugar. Place on cookie sheet about 2" apart. Flatten slightly.
5. Bake 10 minutes. Transfer to cooling rack.

Makes 2½ dozen

HALLOWEEN PEANUT BUTTER FINGERS

½ cup powdered sugar
½ cup powdered milk
⅓ cup + 2 tablespoons peanut butter
⅓ cup + 2 tablespoons light corn syrup
Small stick pretzels
Sliced almonds for fingernails

1. In mixer bowl, combine powdered sugar, milk, peanut butter and syrup. Mix well to form a dough. It will be similar to play dough.
2. Form some dough around each pretzel to create a finger shape. Add an almond for the fingernail. Score with a knife for the knuckles.
3. Keep refrigerated until time to serve. This ghoulish Halloween treat actually tastes good!

Makes 15

"The heart that loves is always young."

~Greek proverb

LEMON BARS

2 cups flour
½ cup powdered sugar
1 cup butter
4 eggs

2 cups sugar
⅓ cup lemon juice
¼ cup flour
½ teaspoon baking powder

1. Preheat oven to 350 degrees. Spray 9"x 13" pan with cooking spray (or spray pan with cooking spray then line with parchment paper).
2. In mixing bowl, combine 2 cups flour and powdered sugar.
3. Cut in butter with pastry blender. Press into prepared pan. Bake 20 minutes or until lightly browned.
4. Beat eggs. Add sugar, lemon juice, ¼ cup flour and baking powder. Mix well and pour over crust.
5. Bake for 25 minutes longer. Cool.
6. Sift powdered sugar over top.

Makes 2 dozen

For best results, allow to set until thoroughly cool before cutting into squares.

MARSHMALLOW BROWNIES

¼ cup baking cocoa
1½ cups sugar
¾ cup butter, softened
3 eggs
1 cup + 2 tablespoons flour

1½ teaspoons vanilla extract
1¼ cups chopped nuts, optional
1 (10 ounce) package mini marshmallows
Chocolate Frosting

1. Preheat oven to 350 degrees.
2. In mixing bowl, cream cocoa, sugar, butter and eggs.
3. Add flour, vanilla and nuts. Use ungreased 9"x 13" pan or spray pan with cooking spray then line with parchment paper. Spread batter in prepared pan and bake 25 minutes.
4. Remove from oven and scatter marshmallows over top of brownies.
5. Return to oven and bake exactly 3 minutes. Cool one hour.
6. Frost with Chocolate Frosting when cooled. (Cover edges well with frosting.)

Makes 2 dozen

For best results: Let stand overnight after frosting.

Chocolate Frosting:
½ cup butter, softened
1¼ cups powdered sugar
¼ cup cocoa
¼ cup evaporated milk

Combine and beat until smooth.

NO-BAKE CHOCOLATE COOKIES

2 cups sugar
3 tablespoons cocoa
½ cup milk
¼ cup butter

½ cup peanut butter
2 cups quick oats
1 teaspoon vanilla extract

1. Mix sugar, cocoa, milk and butter in heavy saucepan.
2. Bring to a full boil over medium heat and boil one minute.
3. Remove from heat.
4. Add peanut butter, oats and vanilla. Stir until blended.
5. Drop by tablespoons onto wax paper.* Let cool until set.

Makes 2 dozen

*If cookies do not hold their shape when spooned onto paper, beat with spoon for a minute or two until mixture thickens.

OATMEAL RAISIN COOKIES

1 cup butter, softened
1 cup brown sugar, packed
¾ cup white sugar
2 eggs
2 teaspoons vanilla extract
2 cups flour
½ teaspoon salt

1 teaspoon baking soda
1 teaspoon baking powder
1 teaspoon cinnamon
2 ¾ cups quick oats
1 cup raisins
1 cup chopped walnuts, optional

1. Preheat oven to 350 degrees.
2. In mixing bowl, cream butter, sugars, eggs and vanilla.
3. In another bowl, combine flour, salt, soda, baking powder, cinnamon and oats.
4. Add flour mixture gradually to butter mixture and mix until well blended.
5. Stir in raisins and nuts. Roll dough into 1" balls and place on ungreased cookie sheets or line with parchment paper. Flatten slightly.
6. Bake 10 minutes.

Makes 2½ dozen

PEANUT BUTTER BARS

½ cup butter, softened
½ cup sugar
½ cup brown sugar, packed
2 eggs
1 teaspoon vanilla extract
½ cup peanut butter

½ cup flour
½ cup dry milk powder
1 teaspoon baking soda
½ cup quick oats
½ cup peanut butter
Frosting

1. Preheat oven to 325 degrees. Grease 9"x 13" baking pan (or spray pan with cooking spray then line with parchment paper).
2. In mixing bowl, cream butter, sugar and brown sugar.
3. Add eggs, vanilla and ½ cup peanut butter. Mix well.
4. In another bowl, combine flour, dry milk powder, baking soda and oats. Add to creamed mixture and stir until blended.
5. Spread in prepared pan and bake 20 minutes. Cool. It is normal for bars to flatten in center. Trim edges, if desired.
6. Whip ½ cup peanut butter with hand mixer. Spread on bars.
7. Refrigerate until cold. Frost.

Makes 2 dozen

Frosting:
¼ cup butter
3 tablespoons water
2 tablespoons baking cocoa
2 cups powdered sugar
2 teaspoons vanilla extract

1. Place butter, water, and cocoa in saucepan. Bring to a boil.
2. Remove from heat. Mix in powdered sugar. Add vanilla.

PEANUT BUTTER COOKIES

1 cup butter, softened
1 cup peanut butter
1 cup sugar
1 cup brown sugar, packed

2 eggs
2½ cups flour
½ teaspoon baking soda
1 teaspoon baking powder

1. Preheat oven to 350 degrees. Lightly grease cookie sheet or line with parchment paper.
2. In mixing bowl, cream butter, peanut butter, sugar and brown sugar until well blended. Stir in eggs.
3. In another bowl, combine flour, baking soda and baking powder. Stir gradually into sugar mixture.
4. Shape dough into 1½" balls. Place 3 inches apart on cookie sheet.
5. With fork, flatten each cookie in crisscross pattern.
6. Bake 12 minutes or until lightly browned.

Makes 3 dozen

PEANUT BUTTER KISS COOKIES

1. Prepare Peanut Butter Cookie dough. Increase flour to 3 cups.
2. Roll into 1" balls and place on cookie sheet.
3. Bake 10 minutes or until lightly brown and tops crack. (While cookies are baking, unwrap candy kisses.)
4. Remove from oven and immediately press candy kiss in top of each cookie. Candy kiss will soften.
5. Cool cookies on rack until kisses set.

Makes 4 dozen

RASPBERRY THUMBPRINTS

½ cup butter, softened
⅓ cup sugar
¼ teaspoon almond extract

1 cup flour
¼ cup raspberry jam

1. Preheat oven to 350 degrees.
2. Combine butter, sugar, almond extract and flour in mixer bowl.
3. Mix until well blended and forms a ball.
4. Roll into ¾" balls and place on ungreased cookie sheet.
5. Make an indentation in top of each cookie and fill with ½ teaspoon jam.
6. Bake 10 minutes. Edges of cookies will be very lightly browned.
7. Let stand on cookie sheet one minute before removing.

Makes 3½ dozen

"Of all earthly music that which reaches farthest into heaven is the beating of a truly loving heart."
~ Henry Ward Beecher

SNICKERDOODLES

¼ cup butter, softened
¼ cup shortening
¾ cup sugar
1 egg
1½ cups flour

1 teaspoon cream of tartar
1 teaspoon baking soda
⅛ teaspoon salt
1 tablespoon sugar mixed
   with 1 teaspoon cinnamon

1. Preheat oven to 400 degrees.
2. In mixing bowl, cream butter, shortening, sugar and egg.
3. In another bowl, combine flour, cream of tartar, soda and salt.
4. Gradually stir flour mixture into creamed mixture until well blended.
5. Shape into 1" balls and roll in sugar and cinnamon mixture.
6. Place 2" apart on ungreased cookie sheet or cookie sheet lined with parchment paper.
7. Bake 10 minutes or until tops are cracked and cookies are lightly browned. Remove from pan and cool on rack.

Makes 2 dozen

SUGAR COOKIES

1 cup butter, softened	2 tablespoons milk
1½ cups sugar	3¾ cups flour
2 eggs	1 teaspoon salt
1½ teaspoons vanilla extract	1 teaspoon baking powder

1. In mixer bowl, cream butter and sugar.
2. Add eggs, vanilla and milk.
3. In another bowl, combine flour, salt and baking powder. Add gradually to creamed mixture. Mix well. Refrigerate 1 hour.
4. Preheat oven to 375 degrees.
5. Place dough on floured board. Roll ¼" to ½" thick (½" for softer cookies). Cut into shapes with cookie cutters.
6. Place on an ungreased cookie sheet or cookie sheet lined with parchment paper. Bake 8 to 10 minutes or until center is set and not doughy.
7. Cool. Decorate with cookie frosting, pg. 159.

Makes 1½ to 3 dozen

WHITE WEDDING COOKIES

½ cup butter, softened
⅓ cup powdered sugar
1 cup flour

1 cup walnuts, finely chopped
¼ teaspoon vanilla extract
Powdered sugar for rolling

1. Preheat oven to 350 degrees.
2. With mixer, blend butter, 1/3 cup powdered sugar, flour, walnuts and vanilla until well blended and dough is not crumbly.
3. Roll dough into 1" round balls.
4. Bake on ungreased cookie sheet or cookie sheet lined with parchment paper 10 minutes.
5. Cool completely. Roll in powdered sugar.

Makes 2½ dozen

"The sound of a kiss is not so loud as that of a cannon, but its echo lasts a great deal longer."
~ *Oliver Wendell Holmes, Sr.*

Main dishes

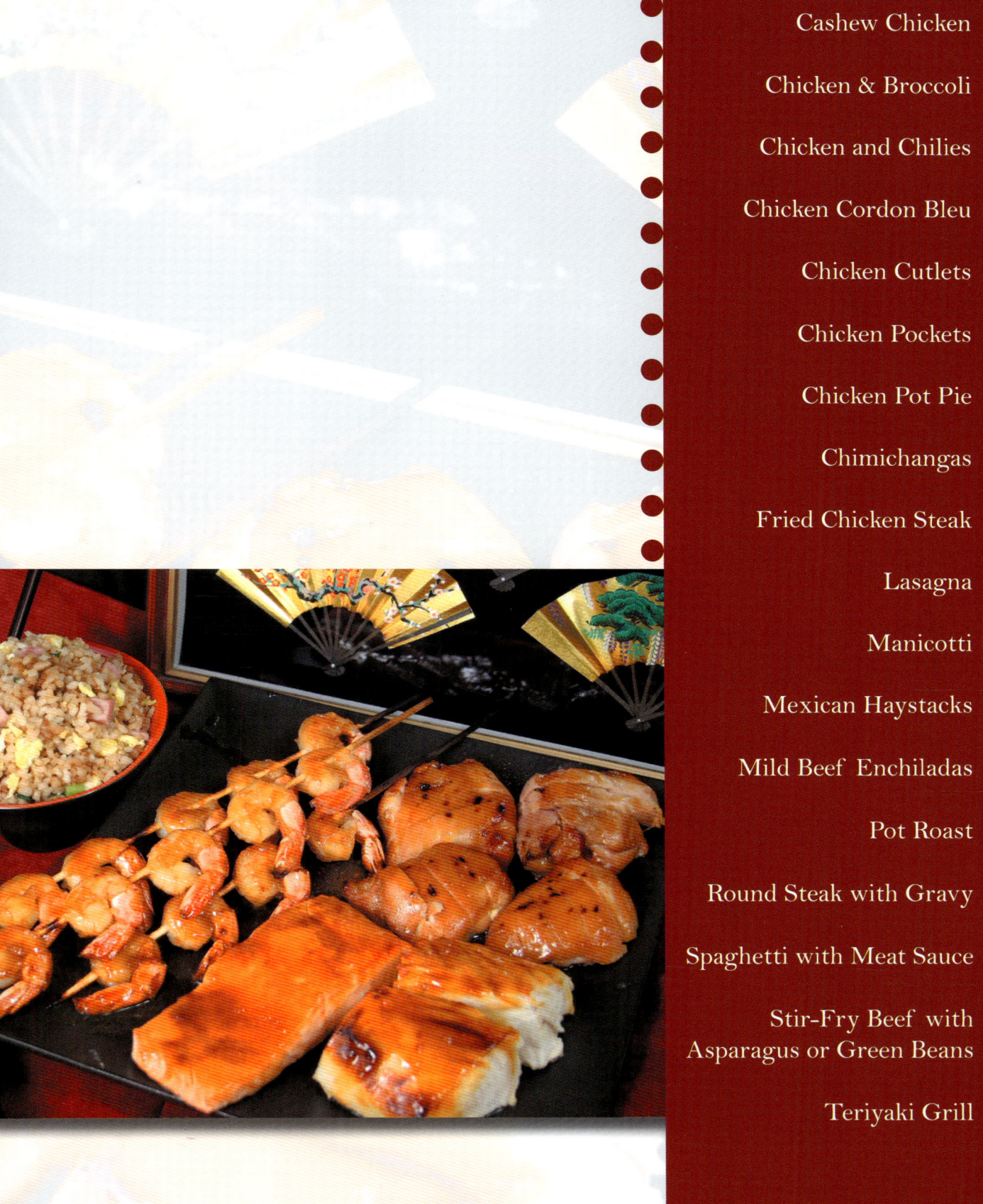

- Cashew Chicken
- Chicken & Broccoli
- Chicken and Chilies
- Chicken Cordon Bleu
- Chicken Cutlets
- Chicken Pockets
- Chicken Pot Pie
- Chimichangas
- Fried Chicken Steak
- Lasagna
- Manicotti
- Mexican Haystacks
- Mild Beef Enchiladas
- Pot Roast
- Round Steak with Gravy
- Spaghetti with Meat Sauce
- Stir-Fry Beef with Asparagus or Green Beans
- Teriyaki Grill

CASHEW CHICKEN

1 tablespoon oil
¼ cup or more cashews
1 chicken breast half, cut in chunks
½ cup chicken broth
2 tablespoons soy sauce
1 tablespoon cornstarch

1 teaspoon sugar
¼ pound Chinese snow peas
¼ pound fresh mushrooms
½ cup celery, sliced or chopped
½ cup carrots, sliced or chopped
2 green onions, sliced

1. In large nonstick pan, heat oil and stir fry cashews on medium heat until lightly toasted. Remove cashews from pan with slotted spoon.
2. In same pan, stir fry chicken until tender and no longer pink in center. Remove chicken from pan with slotted spoon. Remove pan from heat.
3. In a small bowl, combine chicken broth, soy sauce, cornstarch and sugar. Set aside. Return pan to heat.
4. Place snow peas, mushrooms, celery and carrots in pan and stir fry 3 minutes, stirring constantly. Stir in soy sauce mixture. Return chicken to pan.
5. Add green onions and cook until well blended and thickened.
6. Add cashews just before serving.

Makes 4 cups

Serve extra soy sauce on the side, if desired.

CHICKEN AND BROCCOLI

4 boneless chicken breast halves
2 tablespoons oil
Salt and pepper
1 medium bunch broccoli
Sauce
1½ cups cheese, grated

1. Cut chicken in chunks. Heat oil in skillet. Add chicken and sprinkle with salt and pepper.
2. Cook on low heat until chicken is tender and no longer pink in center.
3. Preheat oven to 350 degrees.
4. Wash broccoli. Cut off large stalks and discard. Break or cut broccoli into florets or spears.
5. In saucepan with ¼ cup water, cook broccoli 6 minutes until barely tender. Drain and place in greased 8"x 8" pan.
6. Add chicken. Cover with sauce and top with grated cheese.
7. Bake uncovered 30 minutes or until hot and bubbly.

Serves 4

Sauce:
½ cup mayonnaise
2 (10 ¾ ounce) cans cream of chicken soup
½ tablespoon curry powder, optional
½ tablespoon lemon juice

Mix all ingredients together.

CHICKEN AND CHILIES

2 large boneless chicken breast halves
1 tablespoon oil
2 tablespoons onion, diced
1 (10 ¾ ounce) can cream of chicken soup
2 tablespoons evaporated milk
2 tablespoons diced chilies
2 tablespoons salsa, optional
1 (15 ounce) can chili, optional
4 flour tortillas, broken in pieces
1½ cups Cheddar cheese, grated

1. Preheat oven to 350 degrees. Grease 9" baking dish.
2. Cut chicken into chunks. Heat oil in skillet and add chicken. Cook on medium heat until tender and no longer pink in center.
3. Remove chicken with slotted spoon and place in mixing bowl.
4. Sauté onion in same pan. Add to the chicken.
5. Combine soup, milk, chilies, salsa, chili, tortillas and ½ cup cheese. Mix well and stir into chicken.
6. Pour mixture into prepared baking dish.
7. Cover with foil and bake 15 minutes. Remove foil and sprinkle with remaining 1 cup cheese.
8. Bake uncovered 10 additional minutes or until hot and bubbly.

Serves 4

"Man and wife, being two, are one in love."
~William Shakespeare

CHICKEN CORDON BLEU

4 boneless chicken breast halves
¼ cup seasoned bread crumbs
¼ cup grated Parmesan cheese
4 thin slices of ham
4 strips white cheese,
   (½" thick and 1" long)
½ cup butter, melted

1. Line 9"x 13" baking pan with foil.
2. Place chicken breasts, one at a time, between two sheets wax paper or in a plastic food bag. Gently pound with flat side of meat tenderizer until each is about ¼" thick.
3. Combine bread crumbs and Parmesan cheese. Set aside.
4. On each flattened chicken breast, lay a slice of thin ham.
5. Place a strip of cheese on top of ham at end nearest you. Fold edge of chicken breast over cheese, fold in sides and roll up to enclose the ham and cheese as tightly as possible.
6. Dip each rolled chicken breast in melted butter and roll in bread crumb mixture until evenly coated.
7. Place, seam side down, on prepared pan. Drizzle with remaining melted butter. Cover and refrigerate for at least 4 hours or until next day. Freezes well. (Increase baking time about 15 minutes if frozen.)
8. Preheat oven to 425 degrees.
9. Bake uncovered 25 minutes or until chicken is no longer pink when lightly slashed. Serve with Mornay Sauce.

Serves 4

Mornay Sauce:

2 tablespoons butter
1½ tablespoons flour
¾ cup chicken broth
¾ cup half n' half milk
¼ cup Parmesan cheese, freshly grated

1. In small saucepan, melt butter. Stir in flour.
2. Using whisk, stir in chicken broth and half n' half milk. Bring to a gentle boil. Cook on medium heat, stirring continuously until thickened, about 2 minutes.
3. Add Parmesan cheese. Simmer 2 minutes.

Makes 1½ cups

CHICKEN CUTLETS

4 chicken breast halves
1 cup buttermilk
1 teaspoon garlic powder
½ teaspoon salt
¼ teaspoon pepper
1½ cups dry seasoned bread crumbs
2 tablespoons melted butter

1. Place chicken breasts, one at a time, between two sheets wax paper or in a plastic food bag. Gently pound with flat side of meat tenderizer until each is about ¾" thick. Set aside.
2. In a bowl, mix buttermilk, garlic powder, salt and pepper.
3. Soak chicken in buttermilk mixture for at least 30 minutes. (It is best if placed in refrigerator several hours or overnight.)
4. Preheat oven to 350 degrees. Put chicken in colander briefly to drain excess buttermilk. Chicken should still look coated.
5. Roll chicken pieces in bread crumbs. Place on greased or foil lined cookie sheet.
6. Drizzle with melted butter or lightly apply with pastry brush.
7. Bake uncovered 25 minutes or until chicken is no longer pink in center and crust is browned.

Serves 4

Serving suggestion:
Place a chicken cutlet on a portion of cooked and drained angel hair pasta. Top with chicken gravy or Mornay sauce, pg. 195, and grated Parmesan cheese.

Variations:
- After pounding chicken, dip in beaten egg and roll in seasoned bread crumbs. Place on foil lined baking sheet. Drizzle with melted butter. Bake 350 degrees for 25 minutes.

- Dip in beaten egg, roll in bread crumbs and fry in hot oil. Brown on each side and fry until no longer pink in center.

CHICKEN POCKETS

3 ounces cream cheese
3 tablespoons butter, melted
2 cups cooked chicken
¼ teaspoon salt
⅛ teaspoon pepper
2 tablespoons milk
1 tablespoon chives or green onion, chopped
1 (8 count) can crescent rolls
¾ cup seasoned croutons, crushed
Sauce

1. Soften cream cheese.
2. Preheat oven to 350 degrees. Spray cookie sheet with cooking spray.
3. Combine cream cheese with 2 tablespoons of the melted butter.
4. Shred cooked chicken or cut into small pieces. Add chicken, salt, pepper, milk and chives or green onion.
5. Separate roll dough into 4 squares, pinching together seams.
6. Spoon ¼ the chicken mixture onto each. Fold up, sealing seams with wet fingertips.
7. Brush with remaining 1 tablespoon melted butter and sprinkle with crushed croutons.
8. Bake uncovered for 20 minutes or until golden brown. Top with sauce, if desired.

Makes 4

Sauce:
1 (10 ¾ ounce) can cream of chicken soup
1 cup sour cream
Mix together and heat. Spoon over baked chicken pockets.

For smaller portions:
1. Separate dough into triangles.
2. Use half the amount of chicken mixture to fill.
3. Roll up beginning at wide end of triangle. Seal edges.
4. Bake 10 minutes.

Makes 8

CHICKEN POT PIE

¼ cup butter
½ cup onion, chopped
½ cup celery, chopped
¼ cup flour
2 ¾ cups chicken broth
½ teaspoon salt
¼ teaspoon black pepper
2 cups cooked chicken, chopped
1 cup frozen mixed vegetables, thawed
1 recipe Biscuit dough, pg. 47

1. Preheat oven to 400 degrees. Grease 9" pie plate or several small disposable pie plates.
2. In large skillet melt butter and sauté onion and celery.
3. Add flour and mix well.
4. Slowly stir in chicken broth and cook over medium heat until thick and bubbly.
5. Add salt, pepper, chicken and vegetables.
6. Pour into prepared pie plate. Cut biscuits ½" thick and place 6 on top of the chicken mixture.* (Biscuit dough can be dropped by tablespoons over filling.)
7. Bake uncovered 20 minutes or until biscuits are golden brown.
8. Cool slightly before serving and spoon into individual serving bowls.

Serves 4

*Place extra biscuits on greased baking pan and bake 12 to 15 minutes or until golden brown. Serve with meal or freeze for later use.

> **Beef Pot Pie:**
> Substitute leftover roast beef, cut in chunks, for chicken.

CHIMICHANGAS

1½ pounds beef chuck roast*
½ cup meat drippings
  or beef broth
1 tablespoon flour
½ teaspoon salt
4 (10") flour tortillas

1. Cook roast in crock pot on low 4 hours, or until meat can be easily shredded. Remove meat and shred.
2. Pour drippings from crock pot into measuring cup. Add enough water to make ½ cup broth or use ½ cup beef broth. Pour into medium pot and heat.
3. Whisk in flour and salt. Cook until thickened and stir into the shredded beef.
4. Place scant ½ cup meat mixture on each tortilla.
5. Fold bottom of tortilla up and sides in. Fold top down and secure with toothpick.
6. Fry in ½" deep hot oil until golden brown, then turn over and brown other side. Drain.
7. Serve with fresh tomatoes or canned diced tomatoes with jalapenos, shredded lettuce, grated cheese, sour cream, guacamole or salsa.

Makes 4

*Substitute leftover pot roast, chicken or pork shredded.

"Grow old along with me. The best is yet to be - the last of life for which the first was made."
~Robert Browning

FRIED CHICKEN STEAK

2 chicken breast halves
¼ cup dry bread crumbs
¼ cup grated Parmesan cheese
2 tablespoons vegetable oil

1. Place chicken in plastic food bag and pound with flat side of meat tenderizer to ½" thick. Rinse chicken.
2. Combine bread crumbs and Parmesan cheese. Dip chicken in mixture until well coated.
3. In medium to large frying pan, fry chicken in hot oil. (Oil should cover the bottom of the pan.)
4. Turn steaks over when well browned and brown other side. It takes about 10 minutes per steak to cook through.

Serves 2

Chicken Parmesan
1. Preheat oven to 350 degrees.
2. After frying place Fried Chicken Steaks in 8"x 8" baking dish.
3. Cover with spaghetti sauce or homemade sauce.*
4. Sprinkle with ¼ cup Mozzarella and 1 tablespoon Parmesan cheese.
5. Bake uncovered 20 minutes or until hot and bubbly.

*Sauce:
¼ cup fresh mushrooms, chopped
½ tablespoon butter, melted
Salt & pepper, to taste
½ tablespoon tomato paste
1 cup chicken broth
1 tablespoon cornstarch

1. Brown mushrooms in melted butter. Sprinkle with salt and pepper.
2. Mix in tomato paste and chicken broth. Cook on low heat 25 minutes.
3. Mix cornstarch with two tablespoons water and add to broth mixture. Stir until thickened.

LASAGNA

1 pound lean ground beef
¼ cup onion, chopped
1 teaspoon garlic, minced
1 (15 ounce) can tomatoes
1 package spaghetti sauce mix
1 (6 ounce) can tomato paste
1½ cups water
½ teaspoon garlic powder
½ teaspoon oregano
2½ cups Mozzarella cheese
½ cup Parmesan cheese, grated
1 (8 ounce) carton cottage cheese
6 lasagna noodles

1. To make sauce: In skillet, brown ground beef with onion and garlic. Drain. Add tomatoes, spaghetti sauce mix, tomato paste, water, garlic powder and oregano. Simmer 10 minutes.
2. Preheat oven to 350 degrees. Spray 9"x 9" baking pan with cooking spray.
3. Cook lasagna noodles according to directions on box and drain.
4. Layer ingredients in pan:

    a. Spread 1/3 of the sauce in pan.
    b. Place 3 noodles over sauce. Fold in ends to fit pan.
    c. Cover noodles with ½ carton cottage cheese, ¾ cup Mozzarella cheese and ¼ cup Parmesan cheese.
    d. Repeat steps a through c.
    e. Top with remaining sauce and 1 cup Mozzarella cheese.

    Be sure the last layer of sauce and cheese completely covers the noodles.

5. Bake uncovered for about 40 minutes.

Serves 4

Unbaked lasagna can be frozen for later use. If frozen, take out of freezer 6 hours before baking to thaw.

MANICOTTI

½ (8 ounce) package manicotti pasta (7 tubes)
1 cup cottage cheese
1 cup grated Mozzarella cheese
⅛ cup grated Parmesan cheese
1½ teaspoons parsley flakes
⅛ teaspoon black pepper
1½ cups tomato sauce
Additional ¾ cup Mozzarella cheese for topping

1. Preheat oven to 350 degrees.
2. Cook manicotti pasta according to package directions. Drain. Place on foil or parchment paper to cool.
3. In a large bowl, stir together cheeses, parsley and pepper. (For easier handling, refrigerate at least 15 minutes.) Fill cooled pasta tubes with mixture, using a small spoon.*
4. Spread ½ cup tomato sauce in 7"x 11" oblong baking dish. Arrange filled pasta in a single layer over sauce. Pour 1 cup tomato sauce over pasta and cover with foil. Bake 30 minutes.
5. Remove foil. Top with grated Mozzarella cheese. Bake additional 10 minutes or until cheese is melted.

Serves 4

*Tip: Use large decorator cylinder or disposable pastry bag without a tip to fill the tubes.

Make ahead directions:
1. After assembling manicotti, do not bake.
2. Cover dish tightly with foil, then plastic wrap. Freeze up to two months.
3. Remove plastic wrap; leave tightly covered with foil. Bake 350 degrees for 1½ hours.
4. Remove foil. Add Mozzarella cheese. Bake additional 10 minutes or until cheese is melted.

MEXICAN HAYSTACKS

1½ pounds ground beef
1 (15 ounce) can refried beans
1 (10 ¾ ounce) can cream of mushroom soup
½ cup water
1 (8 ounce) can tomato sauce
1 envelope taco seasoning mix
1 bag tortilla chips

1. In large saucepan, brown ground beef and drain grease.
2. Add refried beans, soup, water, tomato sauce and taco seasoning mix. Mix well. Simmer 15 minutes.
3. Serve over chips. Add Toppings.

Serves 6

Toppings:
Shredded lettuce
Chopped tomato
Sliced olives
Salsa
Sour cream
Grated cheese
Green onion
Guacamole

MILD BEEF ENCHILADAS

1 pound ground beef
  (or cooked, shredded beef)
¼ small onion, chopped
1 (15 ounce) can refried beans,
  optional
½ teaspoon salt
¼ teaspoon pepper
1 (10 ¾ ounce) can cream
  of mushroom soup

1 (10 ounce) can mild
  enchilada sauce
6 (10") flour tortillas
1 cup grated cheese
½ head lettuce, shredded
Sour cream, optional
Guacamole, optional

1. Brown ground beef and onion until meat is no longer pink and onion is tender. Drain. Add refried beans. Season with salt and pepper.
2. Mix together soup and enchilada sauce in saucepan. Heat on medium until hot and bubbly.
3. Spray 9"x 13" pan with cooking spray. Pour half the soup/sauce mixture into bottom of pan. Set aside.
4. Place tortillas on microwave safe plate and cover with paper towel. Heat in microwave 20 seconds.
5. Preheat oven to 350 degrees.
6. Spoon about 3 tablespoons meat on one end of each tortilla. Sprinkle 1 tablespoon cheese over meat. Fold edge of tortilla over filling, tuck sides in and roll up.
7. Place rolled tortillas in pan, seam side down, over sauce. Spread remaining sauce over top, covering tortillas well. Sprinkle with remaining grated cheese.
8. Bake uncovered 25 minutes or until very hot and bubbly. Serve over shredded lettuce and top with sour cream and guacamole.

Makes 6

POT ROAST

1 (3 pound) beef chuck roast
1 envelope onion soup mix
  or other seasoning of choice
6 medium potatoes
1 pound baby carrots
1½ cups beef broth

1. Preheat oven to 325 degrees. Line 9"x 13" baking pan with foil, or use oven bag and follow instructions on package.
2. Place roast in center of pan. Sprinkle with onion soup mix or other seasonings.
3. Scrub potatoes (peel, if desired) and cut in half.
4. Arrange potatoes and carrots around roast. Sprinkle salt or other seasoning over vegetables, if desired.
5. Drizzle beef broth over top. Cover tightly with foil. (Do not cover if using oven bag.)
6. Bake about 4 hours or until meat is tender enough to fall apart when forked.

Serves 6

Crock pot method: Place all ingredients in crock pot and cook according to crock pot instructions. Use slow cooker liners to prevent excessive browning around edges of food and for easier clean up.

Leftovers: Cut meat and vegetables in bite size pieces. Add broth and heat until bubbly for a tasty stew.

Chuck beef cuts are usually economical. They are flavorful and tender when slow cooked. Some popular cuts are:

Chuck Eye Roast   Arm Roast or Round Bone
7 Bone Roast   Cross Rib Roast

ROUND STEAK WITH GRAVY

1½ pound boneless round steak
Flour for coating steak (about ½ cup)
3 tablespoons oil
¼ cup butter
3 tablespoons dry onion soup mix

¼ cup flour
3 cups water
1 tablespoon white vinegar
½ cup mushrooms, sliced

1. Trim fat from steak and discard.
2. Cut steak into serving size pieces. Rinse with water and dip in flour until well coated.
3. Heat oil in skillet. Place steak in hot oil and brown on each side. Remove from pan and set aside.
4. Preheat oven to 300 degrees.
5. To make gravy: Melt butter in same skillet and add onion soup mix. Stir until blended. Add ¼ cup flour and stir well. Using whisk, slowly add water and cook, stirring constantly, until mixture is slightly thickened. Add vinegar and mushrooms.
(Substitute Easy Gravy, if desired)
6. Pour half the gravy in 9"x 9" baking dish. Place browned steak in dish with gravy. Pour remaining gravy over steak.
7. Cover tightly with foil or oven safe lid. Bake 2½ hours.

Serves 4

Easy Gravy:
2 (14 ounce) cans beef broth
4 tablespoons cornstarch
4 tablespoons cold water

1. In saucepan, heat broth.
2. Mix cornstarch and cold water. Stir into broth.
3. Bring to a boil. Pour over meat in casserole dish.

SPAGHETTI WITH MEAT SAUCE

½ pound ground beef
¼ cup onion, chopped
¼ teaspoon garlic powder
1 (6 ounce) can tomato paste
1¼ cups water
1 teaspoon salt
½ teaspoon Worcestershire sauce

2 teaspoons sugar
¼ teaspoon basil
¼ teaspoon black pepper
1½ teaspoons parsley flakes
1 tablespoon Parmesan cheese
1 (6 ounce) package spaghetti or other pasta

1. In saucepan, brown ground beef with onion. Drain.
2. Add garlic powder, tomato paste and water.
3. Add remaining ingredients except pasta.
4. Simmer uncovered 30 minutes.
5. Cook spaghetti or other pasta according to package directions.
6. To serve, top with spaghetti sauce and additional grated Parmesan cheese.

Serves 4

To store cooked spaghetti noodles for later use:
1. After cooking, place in colander and rinse with cold water until spaghetti is cold. Drain well.
2. Toss with 1 tablespoon cooking oil (optional) and place in plastic food storage bag. Seal tightly and refrigerate.
3. When ready to serve, place in colander and rinse with hot water until noodles are hot. Drain well. Serve immediately.

If meatballs are preferred rather than meat sauce:
1. Prepare meatball recipe, page 23.
2. Prepare spaghetti sauce, omitting meat.
3. Add meatballs to sauce while it is simmering.

STIR-FRY BEEF WITH ASPARAGUS

½ cup + 1 tablespoon water
2 tablespoons soy sauce
1 tablespoon cornstarch
⅛ teaspoon black pepper
⅛ teaspoon red cayenne pepper
1 teaspoon garlic, crushed

¾ pound rib eye steak
1 tablespoon oil
½ pound fresh asparagus*
1 (5.95 ounce) can straw mushrooms,** drained

1. Combine water, soy sauce, cornstarch, black pepper, red pepper and garlic. Mix well and set aside.
2. Slice steak thin and stir fry in oil until no longer pink. Remove from skillet.
3. Wash asparagus and break off ends. Leave whole or slice diagonally into 1" pieces. Stir fry until crisp tender.
4. Add soy sauce mixture. Cook about 1 minute or until thickened. Stir in meat and mushrooms.
5. Serve hot over noodles or rice.

Serves 4

*Substitute fresh green beans or broccoli.

**Substitute fresh mushrooms.

"If this be love, don't speak: kisses are all that's needed."
~ Anonymous

TERIYAKI GRILL

Chicken breasts or thighs
Large shrimp, salmon or halibut fillets
Teriyaki sauce or other marinade

1. Chicken:
    a. Cover chicken with teriyaki sauce or other marinade and place in covered container.
    b. Refrigerate several hours or overnight.
    c. Grill or broil until well browned and no longer pink in center. Brush on extra sauce for added flavor.

2. Shrimp:
    a. Use cleaned, de-veined shrimp and thread on wooden skewers which have been soaked in water or on metal skewers.
    b. Grill until browned, brushing each side several times with teriyaki sauce.

3. Salmon or halibut fillets:
    a. Sprinkle lightly with dill and lemon pepper if desired.
    b. Grill or broil until fish flakes with a fork.
    c. Brush with teriyaki sauce the last few minutes of grilling or after removing from heat.

Teriyaki Sauce:

½ cup sugar   2 cups cold water
½ cup soy sauce   2 tablespoons cornstarch

1. In saucepan, combine sugar, soy sauce, cold water and cornstarch. Stir to dissolve sugar. Cook on medium heat until mixture comes to a boil and is thickened, about 2 minutes.
2. Serve with grilled chicken, pork or seafood.

Makes 2 cups

Variation: For Oriental flavor, add ¼ teaspoon crushed garlic and ⅛ teaspoon crushed ginger.

Salads

BBQ Chicken Salad

Broccoli Salad

Chicken Pasta Salad with Fruit

Cobb Salad for Two

Cole Slaw

Country Potato Salad

Crunchy Salad

Lettuce Wedge Salad

Mandarin Green Salad

Mozzarella Tomato Salad

Pasta Salad with Veggies

Platter Salad

Potato Salad

Southwest Salad

Spinach Salad with Strawberries & Pecans

BBQ CHICKEN SALAD

(Prepare chicken and almonds in advance.)
2 chicken breast halves   ¼ cup favorite barbecue sauce
1 tablespoon oil   ½ cup sliced almonds, sugared*

2 cups bagged greens – romaine, mixed, spinach, etc.
¼ cup shredded carrots
¼ cup shredded purple cabbage
½ cup sliced fresh strawberries
1 avocado, peeled and chopped
1 kiwi, peeled and sliced
⅓ cup dried cranberries (near raisins in grocery store)

1. Cut chicken breasts into cubes. In skillet, stir fry in oil until tender and no longer pink in center.
2. Add barbecue sauce, mixing until chicken is well coated. Chill several hours.
3. Wash and drain greens.
4. Add carrots, cabbage, strawberries, avocado, kiwi and cranberries.
5. Add chicken. Serve with poppy seed dressing.
6. Top with sugared almonds.

Serves 4

*Melt 3 tablespoons sugar in heavy saucepan. Stir in sliced almonds. Remove from heat and spread in thin layer on wax paper. Allow to cool completely. Break into small pieces. Sugared almonds freeze well. (Packaged sugared nuts can be found in most grocery stores.)

Light Poppy Seed Dressing:
½ cup light mayonnaise   ¼ cup sugar
1 tablespoon vinegar   ½ teaspoon poppy seeds

Mix ingredients and refrigerate until ready to serve.

BROCCOLI SALAD

2 cups chopped fresh broccoli
1/3 cup sunflower kernels, salted and roasted
2 bacon strips, fried crisp and crumbled
Dressing
Red onion slices, optional

1. Combine broccoli and sunflower kernels.
2. Stir in crumbled bacon and dressing* just before serving.
3. Garnish with red onion slices, if desired.

Serves 4

*Dressing should be added to individual portions just before serving to prevent wilting. Any leftover salad should be stored without dressing added.

Creamy Salad Dressing:
1/4 cup mayonnaise   1 1/2 tablespoons sugar
1/8 teaspoon salt   1/2 tablespoon white or rice vinegar

Blend all ingredients. Keep refrigerated.

CHICKEN PASTA SALAD WITH FRUIT

1 chicken breast half
1½ cups uncooked pasta
⅓ cup chopped celery
1 cup fruit of choice*

½ cup coleslaw dressing or Lime Tarragon Salad dressing
⅓ cup cashews or slivered almonds

1. Cut chicken into bite-size chunks. Sauté in small amount of oil until tender and no longer pink in center. Refrigerate until cold.
2. Cook pasta of choice according to package directions. Pour into colander and drain. Rinse with ice cold water until cooled. Combine pasta, chicken, celery, and fruits. Refrigerate until well chilled.
3. Just before serving, mix dressing into chicken mixture. Top with cashews or slivered almonds.

Serves 4

*Suggested fruits: pineapple tidbits, mango, grapes, avocado

Lime Tarragon Salad Dressing:

¼ cup mayonnaise
1½ teaspoons sugar
⅛ teaspoon salt
1½ teaspoons vinegar

1½ teaspoons lime juice
1 tablespoon milk
½ teaspoon tarragon
⅛ teaspoon mustard, optional

1. Mix all ingredients and refrigerate until chilled.
2. Toss into salad prior to serving.
3. Top with cashews or slivered almonds.

COBB SALAD FOR TWO

¼ head iceberg lettuce

1. Wash lettuce and break into bite-size pieces.
2. Place lettuce in serving bowl and top with choice of ingredients:

1 cup cooked, diced chicken (one chicken breast half)
2 boiled eggs, sliced
1 small avocado, peeled and chopped
1 medium tomato, chopped
6 cooked, peeled shrimp or ½ cup salad shrimp
¼ cup crumbled bleu cheese
4 slices cooked, crumbled bacon
Chopped green onion

Serves 2

Thousand Island Dressing:
½ cup mayonnaise
2 tablespoons ketchup
1 tablespoon pickle relish

Mix together until well blended.

COLE SLAW

4 cups cabbage, diced*
½ cup carrots, diced*
1 tablespoon onion, minced
¼ cup milk
1 tablespoon white vinegar

1 tablespoon lemon juice
¼ cup mayonnaise
2 tablespoons sugar
¼ teaspoon black pepper
½ teaspoon salt

1. In a mixing bowl, combine cabbage, carrots and onion. Set aside.
2. In another bowl, blend together milk, vinegar, lemon juice, mayonnaise, sugar, pepper and salt. Stir with whisk until well blended.
3. Pour over cabbage mixture and toss well with fork.
4. Cover. Refrigerate until well chilled, about 2 hours.

Serves 4

*Substitute packaged coleslaw mix.

Tip: Substitute 1/3 cup buttermilk for milk, vinegar, and lemon juice.

"I want to marry someone like my daddy 'cause he's handsomer than a prince."

~Emma, Age 5

COUNTRY POTATO SALAD

4 medium potatoes
½ tablespoon salt
¼ small onion, diced
1 large dill pickle, diced

3 boiled eggs, chopped
½ teaspoon seasoned salt
⅛ teaspoon pepper
1 cup mayonnaise or more

1. Cook potatoes by desired method:

   - Place scrubbed potatoes in kettle. Cover with water. Add salt.
   - Bring to gentle boil and cook until potatoes fork tender.
   - Remove from heat, drain and let sit until cooled off enough to handle.
   - Peel potatoes and cut into cubes.

     - Or -

   - Peel and cut potatoes into cubes. Place in kettle. Cover with water.
   - Add salt. Cook until potatoes are tender.
   - Remove and drain. Cool.*

2. Place cooked potatoes, onion, pickles and eggs in large bowl. Toss together with large fork.
3. Add seasoned salt and pepper.
4. Carefully stir in mayonnaise until well blended.
5. Refrigerate. Add additional mayonnaise if needed.

Serves 4

*For mashed potato salad, mix while potatoes are still very warm.

CRUNCHY SALAD

¼ head iceberg lettuce
1 (10 ounce) package frozen peas, thawed
1 (6 ounce) can sliced water chestnuts, drained
½ cup celery, diced
¼ cup mayonnaise
½ cup sour cream
3 tablespoons grated cheese, Parmesan or Monterey Jack
4 slices bacon, fried, crisp and crumbled

1. Wash lettuce with cold water. Drain well or spin in salad spinner. Break into bite size pieces.
2. Place in bottom of 1 quart salad bowl. (Looks pretty in a clear bowl.)
3. On top of lettuce, layer peas, water chestnuts and celery.
4. In small bowl, mix mayonnaise and sour cream. Spread over vegetables. Sprinkle cheese and bacon on top.
5. Cover with plastic wrap and refrigerate overnight.

Serves 6

LETTUCE WEDGE SALAD

¼ head iceberg lettuce
2 small tomatoes
2 slices bacon, fried crisp
Chunky Bleu Cheese Dressing

1. Remove core from lettuce head and wash under cold running water.
2. Place on cutting board and cut a wedge from the head, about ¼ of the lettuce head. Cut wedge in half, making 2 wedges.
3. Place each of the two wedges in a shallow salad bowl. (Bag and refrigerate remaining lettuce for later use.)
4. Cut tomatoes into wedges and add to plate. Crumble and add bacon.
5. Top lettuce wedge with 2 tablespoons bleu cheese dressing.
6. Garnish with bleu cheese crumbles.

Serves 2

Chunky Bleu Cheese Dressing:
½ cup mayonnaise
½ cup sour cream
2 ounces bleu cheese, crumbled
½ teaspoon Worcestershire sauce
¼ teaspoon garlic powder

1. Combine all ingredients.
2. This makes a thick dressing. For thinner dressing, add a little milk.

Makes 1 cup

MANDARIN GREEN SALAD

¼ cup sliced almonds
1½ tablespoons sugar
¼ head iceberg lettuce
½ head romaine lettuce

1 celery rib (about ½ cup), sliced
2 green onions, chopped, optional
1 (11 ounce) can mandarin oranges, well drained

1. Mix almonds and sugar in heavy saucepan. Cook on medium heat, stirring constantly, until sugar melts and almonds are coated.
2. Remove from heat and spread in thin layer on wax paper.
3. Cool and break into small pieces.
4. Cut lettuce and place in a large salad bowl. Add celery and onions.
5. Add almonds, oranges and dressing* just before serving.

Serves 4

*Lettuce wilts quickly once dressing is added. Add dressing to individual portions just before serving. Store leftover salad without dressing added.

Oil Vinegar Dressing:
2 tablespoons oil
1 tablespoon sugar
1 tablespoon vinegar
½ tablespoon snipped parsley (or 1 teaspoon dried)
¼ teaspoon salt
⅛ teaspoon pepper
⅛ teaspoon Tabasco,

Place in shaker container and shake until blended. Chill.

MOZZARELLA TOMATO SALAD

8 ounces fresh Mozzarella cheese
2 large tomatoes
8 fresh basil leaves
2 tablespoons extra virgin olive oil
2 tablespoons balsamic vinegar

1. Slice cheese into ¼" slices. Slice tomatoes. Wash and drain basil leaves.
2. Alternate cheese slices, tomato slices and basil leaves on a round 10" plate or platter. Sprinkle lightly with salt and pepper.
3. Mix olive oil and vinegar. Pour over salad, as desired. Reserve extra dressing for dipping bread.

Serves 2

Serving suggestion: Crusty Italian bread is delicious with this salad!

"*My heart is ever at your service.*"

~William Shakespeare

PASTA SALAD WITH VEGGIES

½ pound (8 ounce) rainbow pasta
1 carrot, thinly sliced
1 small zucchini, thinly sliced
1 cup fresh broccoli pieces
¼ pound fresh mushrooms, sliced

1 (6 ounce) can sliced black olives
1 tomato, diced
1 cup ranch dressing
¼ cup Italian dressing

1. Cook pasta according to directions on package.
2. Rinse in cold water. Drain.
3. Wash and cut vegetables. Place in a large bowl.
4. Add cooked pasta and salad dressings.
5. Toss and refrigerate for several hours or overnight.

Serves 6

This recipe can be tailored to your personal tastes:
- substitute any favorite raw veggies.
- substitute other types of pasta for the rainbow pasta.
- add ham and/or cheese cubes

PLATTER SALAD

¼ head red leaf lettuce
¼ head green leaf lettuce
¼ head iceberg lettuce
¼ pound bacon

¼ cup Mozzarella cheese
4 ounces cottage cheese
Purple onion slices for garnish
Poppy Seed Dressing

1. Line a plate or platter with red and green leaf lettuce.
2. Break up remaining leaf lettuce and iceberg lettuce. Place over lettuce leaves on platter.
3. Fry bacon until crisp and drain on paper towels. Break into pieces.
4. Scatter bacon pieces, Mozzarella cheese and cottage cheese over lettuce. Arrange slices of purple onion over top.
5. Serve with dressing.

Serves 6

Poppy Seed Dressing:

½ cup mayonnaise
¼ cup sugar
½ tablespoon poppy seeds
1½ tablespoons white vinegar

Whisk all ingredients together. Chill.

POTATO SALAD

2 teaspoons flour
1 tablespoon warm water
¼ teaspoon dry mustard
¼ teaspoon salt
¼ teaspoon prepared mustard
¼ cup hot water
¼ cup apple cider vinegar

2 tablespoons sugar
¾ cup salad dressing
3 eggs, hard boiled and cooled
4 medium potatoes
¼ cup dill pickles, chopped (optional)
¼ cup onion, chopped (optional)

1. In a bowl, mix flour, warm water, dry mustard, salt and mustard.
2. In saucepan, combine hot water, vinegar and sugar. Bring to a boil.
3. Using a whisk, add flour mixture to sugar mixture and stir briskly until well mixed and thickened. Remove from heat.
4. Add salad dressing. Mix well and refrigerate.
5. Peel and chop potatoes. In saucepan, cover potatoes with water and cook until tender. Drain. Place in salad bowl.
6. Peel eggs and coarsely chop.* Add to potatoes. Cover potatoes and eggs. Cool in refrigerator.
7. Stir dressing mixture, pickles and onion into potatoes and eggs. Refrigerate until ready to serve.

Serves 4

Slice 1 egg to garnish top.

The dressing for this salad is also good for mixing with diced or ground ham for ham salad sandwiches.

SOUTHWEST SALAD

2 chicken breast halves
1 tablespoon taco seasoning
½ cup rice, uncooked
1 teaspoon lime juice
½ cup cheese, shredded

2 (10") flour tortillas
½ cup black beans
½ cup lettuce, shredded
Salsa Fresh
Cilantro Dressing

1. Cut chicken breast into small cubes. Stir fry in 1 tablespoon oil until done. Mix in taco seasoning. Drain. Cover and refrigerate.
2. Prepare rice (not instant) according to package directions or prepare in microwave rice cooker according to cooker instructions. Stir in lime juice.
3. Place shredded cheese on tortillas. Place under broiler briefly until cheese melts and edges begin to brown (watch closely).
4. Top baked tortilla with prepared rice, black beans, prepared chicken, shredded lettuce, fresh salsa and cilantro buttermilk dressing.

Makes 2 large salads

This salad is quick to make if chicken, rice and cilantro dressing are prepared and refrigerated in advance.

Cilantro Buttermilk Dressing:

1 packet ranch dressing mix
1 cup mayonnaise
½ cup buttermilk
½ teaspoon garlic, minced

1 cup cilantro, chopped
3 tomatillos, crushed, or
¼ cup salsa verde
⅛ teaspoon cayenne pepper

Mix all ingredients in blender. Refrigerate.

SPINACH SALAD WITH STRAWBERRIES AND PECANS

1 (6 ounce) package fresh baby spinach
1 cup strawberries, cut in half
½ cup toasted pecans

1. Rinse spinach and place in 2 salad bowls.
2. Top with sliced strawberries and pecans.
3. Cover and refrigerate until ready to serve.
4. Serve with poppy seed dressing.

Makes 2 large salads

Light Poppy Seed Dressing:
½ cup light mayonnaise
1 tablespoon vinegar
¼ cup sugar
½ teaspoon poppy seeds

Mix ingredients and refrigerate until ready to serve.

Sandwiches

BBQ Pork Sandwich

California Wrap

Chicken Salad Sandwich

Chili Dogs

Club Sandwich

Egg Salad Sandwich

French Dip

Monterey Chicken Croissants

Patty Melt

BBQ PORK SANDWICHES

4 boneless pork ribs (1½ pounds)
Salt and pepper
BBQ Sauce, homemade
  (Or use favorite bottled barbecue sauce)
4 large seeded buns

1. Season meat with salt and pepper.
2. Place in baking pan and seal tightly with foil.
3. Bake 250 degrees 3 hours, or until tender enough to shred with a fork.
4. After shredding meat, drain and add to sauce.
5. Serve on seeded buns.

Makes 4

BBQ Sauce:

¼ cup onion, finely diced
1 tablespoon butter
1 cup ketchup
½ cup water
1 tablespoon liquid smoke

2 tablespoons Worcestershire
½ teaspoon garlic powder
¼ teaspoon cumin powder
½ tablespoon white vinegar
1 tablespoon brown sugar

1. In saucepan, sauté onion in melted butter.
2. Add all other ingredients. Simmer about 5 minutes.

Makes 1½ cups

CALIFORNIA WRAP

2 (10") large tortillas
4 teaspoons Thousand Island dressing (or dressing of choice)
6 thin slices turkey*
4 thin slices cheese

4 slices bacon, fried crisp
2 lettuce leaves
½ tomato, cut in wedges
½ avocado, sliced

1. Soften tortillas in microwave for 10 seconds each.
2. Spread dressing, to taste, on each tortilla.
3. Leaving 1" border around the tortilla, place 3 turkey slices on each.
4. Add 2 cheese slices and 2 slices bacon.
5. Top with lettuce, tomato and avocado.
6. Add extra dressing, if desired.
7. Roll end closest to you over the filling. Fold in one end to hold filling in place and finish rolling. Secure with toothpick.

Makes 2

*Substitute 1 cooked chicken breast half (grilled, broiled or baked), cut into lengthwise strips.

CHICKEN SALAD SANDWICHES

2 cups cooked chicken
¼ cup mayonnaise
½ tablespoon lemon juice
¼ teaspoon salt
⅛ teaspoon black pepper
¼ cup celery, diced
Leafy lettuce
12 dollar rolls or mini croissants

1. Chop or shred cooked chicken.
2. Combine mayonnaise, lemon juice, salt, pepper and celery.
3. Stir in chicken until all ingredients are well blended.
4. Refrigerate until ready to serve.
5. To serve, place piece of leafy lettuce on mini roll or croissant and add heaping tablespoon chicken salad.

Makes 12

Variation: Add ¼ cup toasted, slivered almonds to chicken mixture.

Chicken Salad: Add grapes and slivered almonds and serve on lacy lettuce leaf.

"There is nothing more admirable than two people who see eye-to-eye keeping house as man and wife, confounding their enemies, and delighting their friends."

~Homer, 9th Century BC

CHILI DOGS

½ pound lean ground beef
½ cup ketchup
½ cup water
½ teaspoon chili powder, or to taste
1 tablespoon quick oats
½ teaspoon salt, or to taste
4 cooked wieners
4 hot dog buns

1. Place ground beef in small pot and mash with potato masher.
2. Cook on medium heat until lightly browned.
3. Add ketchup, water, chili powder, oats and salt. Mix well.
4. Cook over low to medium heat until mixture is thickened, approximately 10 minutes.
5. Place cooked wieners in buns and top with chili mixture.

Makes 4

Chili dogs:
Place wieners in buns and top with chili. Serve with mustard and chopped onion.

Southern style hot dogs:
Place wieners in buns and top with chili, chopped onion, ketchup, mustard and mayonnaise, as desired.

CLUB SANDWICH

6 slices sandwich bread
2 teaspoons mayonnaise
6 thin slices deli turkey
6 thin slices deli ham
4 slices bacon, fried crisp

2 slices white cheese
2 slices yellow cheese
2 lettuce leaves, washed
  and drained
1 small tomato, sliced

1. Toast bread until golden brown.
2. Spread mayonnaise on one side of each slice bread.
3. Roll deli meats, if desired.
4. To assemble: layer meats, sliced cheeses, lettuce and tomato on bread, using three slices bread for each sandwich (one slice for top, one slice for bottom and third slice in middle of sandwich).
5. Cut sandwich into fourths. Secure each fourth with toothpick.

Makes 2

EGG SALAD SANDWICH

3 large eggs
1 or 2 tablespoons mayonnaise
1 tablespoon sweet pickle relish
4 thick slices whole wheat bread
Lettuce and tomato, optional

1. Place eggs in small saucepan. Cover with water.
2. Bring to a full boil and boil 10 minutes.
3. Drain water and run cold water over eggs. Let sit in cold water until eggs are cooled.
4. Remove shells and mash eggs with fork.
5. Add mayonnaise and pickle relish. Mix lightly.
6. Spread on bread. Add lettuce and tomato, if desired.

Makes 2

FRENCH DIP

1 long French roll
6 slices deli roast beef
2 slices Swiss cheese

2 cups Au Jus gravy*
or beef broth

1. Toast French roll, if desired.
2. Pile roast beef and cheese on roll.
3. Slice in half. Dip in gravy.

Makes 1 large sandwich

*Au jus mix packets can be found in most grocery stores. Prepare according to directions on packet.

"If you build a castle in the air....That is where they should be. Now put the foundation under them."
~Henry David Thoreau

MONTEREY CHICKEN CROISSANTS

4 chicken breast halves
2 cups bottled ranch dressing
4 slices Monterey Jack cheese
½ ripe avocado, sliced
1 tomato, sliced
4 croissants

1. Preheat oven to 250 degrees.
2. Place chicken breasts in roasting pan.* Cover with ranch dressing and bake, covered, for 2½ hours.
3. Slice croissants. Place a chicken breast and cheese slice on each croissant.
4. Top with tomato and avocado. Spoon on ranch dressing.

Makes 4

*Cook chicken in crock pot on low for 2 to 3 hours until tender or cook chicken in covered skillet on stovetop at medium heat until chicken is tender.

PATTY MELT

2 slices French bread
   or sourdough bread
¼ pound lean hamburger patty
1 thick slice Swiss cheese
   or cheese of choice

2 slices onion, grilled
Mayonnaise
   or salad dressing
Ketchup
Pickles

1. Butter and grill bread until toasted.
2. Pan-fry hamburger patty until no longer pink in center.
3. Place cheese on patty in pan, turn off heat and cover with lid until cheese begins to melt or place patty with cheese in microwave until cheese melts.
4. Place on one slice of bread and top with onion.
5. Garnish with mayo, ketchup and pickles, to taste.
6. Top with remaining slice of bread.

Makes 1 large sandwich

Side dishes

Baked Beans

Baked Potatoes

Carrot Casserole

Cheddar Fries

Company Potatoes

Creamy Mashed Potatoes

Deviled Eggs

Fried Cauliflower

Glazed Carrots

Green Beans
with Slivered Almonds

Pasta Alfredo

Rice Pilaf

Sautéed Mushrooms

Spaghetti Squash

Spanish Rice

Stir-Fried Rice

Stir-Fry Vegetable Medley

Twice Baked Potatoes

BAKED BEANS

4 slices bacon
¼ pound ground beef, optional
2 tablespoons onion, diced
¼ green bell pepper, diced
1 cup canned tomatoes, diced
¼ cup brown sugar, packed

2 tablespoons molasses
⅛ teaspoon salt
⅛ teaspoon black pepper
½ teaspoon chili powder
1 (15 ounce) can pork n' beans
   or white navy beans

1. In skillet, fry bacon until crisp. Crumble and set aside.
2. In large saucepan, brown ground beef, onion and green pepper. Drain grease.
3. Add tomatoes, brown sugar, molasses, salt, black pepper and chili powder. Stir in beans and prepared bacon.
4. Cook on low heat 1 hour or longer until well blended and thick.

Serves 4

"People are just about as happy as they make up their minds to be."

~ Abraham Lincoln

BAKED POTATOES

[photo on page 204]

2 medium potatoes, unpeeled
Shortening or Oil

1. Preheat oven to 350 degrees.
2. Scrub potatoes with vegetable brush. Pierce with fork. Rub with shortening or oil.
3. Place on center rack of oven and bake 60 to 80 minutes until potatoes fork tender. Cool slightly.
4. Roll in hands to loosen inside of potato. Cut crisscross on top. Press ends and push up to fluff. Serve with desired toppings.

Foil wrapped potatoes:
1. Preheat oven to 350 degrees.
2. Scrub and dry potatoes.
3. Wrap each potato in foil. Bake 60 to 80 minutes until potatoes fork tender. Serve with desired toppings.

Toppings:		
butter	grated cheese	sour cream
salt & pepper	chives	bacon crumbles

Baked sweet potatoes: (photo opposite page)
1. Preheat oven to 350 degrees. Scrub and dry potatoes.
2. Pierce each potato several times with fork.
3. Place piece of foil on lower rack to catch drips.
4. Bake 60 to 90 minutes until potatoes fork tender. Serve with maple or brown sugar butter.

Serves 2

Maple Butter:	Brown Sugar Butter:
2 tablespoons maple syrup	2 tablespoons butter, softened
4 tablespoons butter, softened	1 tablespoon brown sugar, packed
Combine and blend until smooth.	Combine and blend until smooth.

CARROT CASSEROLE

4 medium carrots, peeled and sliced
2 tablespoons onion, minced
1 tablespoon butter
1½ tablespoons flour
¼ teaspoon salt
⅛ teaspoon dry mustard
⅛ teaspoon celery salt
1 cup milk
⅛ teaspoon black pepper
1 cup Cheddar cheese, grated
1 cup soft bread crumbs

1. In saucepan, cover carrots with water and cook until barely tender, about 20 minutes. Drain.
2. Grease 1 quart casserole dish. Preheat oven to 350 degrees.
3. White sauce: In saucepan, sauté onion in butter. Add flour, salt, dry mustard and celery salt. Gradually add milk and pepper. Stir until thickened.
4. Place cooked carrots in dish. Add cheese and white sauce. Sprinkle with bread crumbs.
5. Bake 25 minutes or until bread crumbs are nicely browned.

Serves 2

CHEDDAR FRIES

2 large baking potatoes
½ cup flour
½ teaspoon seasoned salt
½ teaspoon garlic salt
½ cup water

2 cups oil
1½ cups Cheddar cheese, shredded
Fry sauce

1. Cut fries ¼" to ½" thick and place in a bowl of cold water to prevent potatoes from turning brown.
2. With whisk combine flour, seasoned salt, garlic salt and water. (Add a little more water if needed to thin mixture to consistency of pancake batter.)
3. Place oil in medium saucepan over medium heat.
4. Test oil with a drop of batter. If it immediately rises to top, oil is ready. If drop turns black, reduce heat.
5. Drain potatoes and pat dry. Dip in batter until well coated.
6. Using tongs, lower fries one at a time into hot oil. Separate any fries that stick together. Fry until light to medium brown. Drain on paper towels.
7. Place fries in 8" baking dish. Add 1 cup shredded cheese and toss. Top with ½ cup cheese or more and microwave about 2 minutes or until cheese melts.

Serves 2

Fry Sauce:
½ cup mayonnaise
2 tablespoons ketchup
¼ teaspoon cayenne pepper

For Seasoned Fry Sauce, add:
½ teaspoon sugar
¼ teaspoon seasoned salt
⅛ teaspoon garlic salt

1. Combine all ingredients. Mix well.
2. Serve with hot fries.

COMPANY POTATOES

3 medium potatoes, not peeled
2 tablespoons butter
1 (10 ¾ ounce) can cream of chicken soup
½ cup sour cream
¾ cup Cheddar cheese, grated
2 tablespoons green onion
Salt and pepper
¾ cup cornflake crumbs
1 tablespoon melted butter

1. Boil potatoes until fork tender. Cool and remove skins. Dice or grate into a large bowl.
2. Preheat oven to 350 degrees. Grease 8" baking dish.
3. In saucepan, heat 2 tablespoons butter and soup.
4. Add sour cream and pour over potatoes. Stir well.
5. Mix in cheese. Chop green onion and add.
6. Season with salt and pepper, to taste. Stir well.
7. Spread into prepared baking dish. Bake 20 minutes, uncovered.
8. Mix cornflake crumbs and melted butter. Sprinkle over top of potatoes and bake an additional 10 minutes.

Serves 6

"To get the full value of joy, you must have someone to divide it with."

~*Mark Twain*

CREAMY MASHED POTATOES

[photo on page 216]

4 medium potatoes, peeled and cubed
1 teaspoon salt
2 tablespoons butter, softened
1 tablespoon milk
3 ounces cream cheese, soft

1. Place potatoes in saucepan and cover with water.
2. Add salt and boil gently until potatoes are tender and break easily when pierced with fork. Drain.
3. Place potatoes in mixer bowl. Add butter, milk and cream cheese. Beat until fluffy.
4. Serve hot with gravy.
5. Keeps well in refrigerator for several days.*
6. To freeze: Place in freezer container and seal well. Thaw and heat when ready to use.

Serves 4

*Leftover mashed potatoes can be used in potato roll recipe.

Plain Mashed Potatoes:
Omit cream cheese and increase milk to 3 tablespoons.

Garlic Potatoes:
To Step 3, add 1 teaspoon crushed garlic and sprinkle top with ¼ cup freshly grated Parmesan cheese.

DEVILED EGGS

2 eggs
4 teaspoons mayonnaise
¼ teaspoon mustard, optional
Salt and pepper
Paprika

1. Place eggs in small saucepan and cover with water. Have water 1" above eggs. Bring to a full boil over medium high heat.
2. Turn off heat, cover, and let stand 15 minutes for hard boiled.*
3. Remove eggs from water and place in a bowl of ice water. Let stand 2 minutes. Peel under cold running water.
4. Cut each egg in half, lengthwise, and scoop out the yolk. Place egg whites on plate.
5. Place yolks in bowl and mash. Stir in mayonnaise, adding more if yolks are too dry.
6. Add small amount of mustard, to taste, if desired.
7. Season with salt and pepper. Mix well.
8. Fill each egg white half with egg yolk mixture. Sprinkle with paprika.

Makes 4

*This method of cooking eggs is called "steeping." The eggs are less likely to develop a green edge around the yolk if cooked by this method.

To cook eggs by standard method:
1. Cover eggs with water and bring to a full boil.
2. Boil gently 10 minutes.
3. Drain water and place eggs in cold water until cool enough to peel.

FRIED CAULIFLOWER

½ small head cauliflower, about 3 cups
1 egg
½ cup flour*
Salt and pepper to taste
¼ cup vegetable oil

1. Cut cauliflower in half. Wrap unused portion and store in refrigerator.
2. Remove stems from cauliflower and break florets into small pieces.
3. Place pieces in colander and wash thoroughly.
4. Break egg into medium bowl and beat with whisk. Add cauliflower to egg and toss until all pieces are coated. Remove from egg and place in colander to drain.
5. Measure flour, salt and pepper into plastic freezer bag. Add cauliflower. Seal top of bag and shake to dust all the florets.
6. Pour cauliflower pieces from bag into dry colander. Shake lightly to remove excess flour.
7. In 12" skillet, fry in hot oil until golden brown.
8. Reduce heat to low. Cover pan and continue to cook on low heat until tender but not mushy. Remove lid and fry for few more minutes.
9. Drain on paper towels. Serve hot.

Serves 4

*Replace flour with dry bread crumbs, if desired.

GLAZED CARROTS

5 carrots (about ½ pound)
1 tablespoon butter
1 tablespoon sugar

⅛ teaspoon ginger
   or nutmeg
½ teaspoon salt

1. Peel carrots and slice on bias. Place in medium saucepan.
2. Add just enough water to cover carrots.
3. Place lid on saucepan and bring to a full boil. Lower heat to medium and continue to cook covered until carrots fork tender, about 5 minutes. Drain.
4. Add butter, sugar, ginger or nutmeg and salt to carrots.
5. Stir over low heat until carrots are glossy.

Serves 2

"Marriage: The keeper of love's promises."

~ *Judy Williams*

GREEN BEANS WITH SLIVERED ALMONDS

½ pound fresh green beans
2 slices bacon
2 tablespoons slivered almonds

1. Wash green beans and remove ends.
2. Place beans in saucepan and cover with hot water. Boil 5 minutes. Drain.
3. In skillet, fry bacon on low heat until crisp and remove from pan. Drain on paper towel.
4. Stir-fry almonds in bacon grease until light golden color.
5. Remove with slotted spoon and drain on paper towel.
6. Stir-fry green beans in bacon grease until hot and crisp tender, about 2 minutes.
7. Crumble bacon over beans and top all with the toasted almonds.

Serves 2

PASTA ALFREDO

4 large mushrooms, sliced
2 tablespoons butter
2 tablespoons flour
½ teaspoon salt
1 cup chicken broth
½ cup milk
½ cup Parmesan cheese, shredded
¼ teaspoon black pepper
1 teaspoon parsley flakes
½ (8 ounce) box fettuccine or linguine

1. In skillet, sauté mushrooms in butter on medium high heat. Whisk in flour and salt.
2. Gradually whisk in chicken broth and milk. Simmer 5 to 10 minutes or until gravy-like thickness. Stir in Parmesan cheese.
3. Add pepper and parsley flakes. Let simmer 15 minutes.
4. Cook pasta according to package directions. Drain.
5. Serve sauce over pasta.

Serves 2

Chicken Alfredo:
1. Grill and season 1 chicken breast half.
2. Cut into strips.
3. Place on noodles just before adding sauce.

RICE PILAF

1 tablespoon butter
¼ small onion, minced
⅛ cup celery, finely chopped
½ cup uncooked rice

1½ cups chicken broth
½ tablespoon dry parsley flakes
⅛ cup slivered almonds, toasted*

1. Preheat oven to 325 degrees. Grease 8″ casserole dish.
2. Melt butter in skillet. Add onion and celery. Sauté 2 minutes.
3. Spread rice in prepared baking dish and add broth.
4. Scatter sautéed onion and celery over broth.
5. Cover and bake 30 minutes or until liquid is absorbed and rice is tender.
6. Just before serving, add parsley and almonds. Toss lightly.

Serves 4

*To toast almonds:
Preheat oven to 350 degrees.
Spread almonds in single layer on ungreased cookie sheet.
Bake 5 minutes, stirring occasionally, until lightly browned.

SAUTÉED MUSHROOMS

1 cup button mushrooms, fresh
1 tablespoon butter

1. Wash mushrooms.
2. Melt butter in skillet.
3. Add mushrooms and stir-fry until mushrooms are lightly browned.

Serves 2

"A house is made of bricks and beams. A home is made of Love and Dreams."
~ *Anonymous*

SPAGHETTI SQUASH

1 (2 pound) spaghetti squash
butter and salt, to taste

1. Preheat oven to 350 degrees.
2. Wash unpeeled squash. Pierce all over with a fork.
3. Place on foil lined cookie sheet and bake 1 to 1½ hours.
4. After baking, cut squash in half, scrape out seeds with large spoon.
5. Separate into strands with a fork.
6. Season with butter and salt.

Serves 4

SPANISH RICE

2 cups long grain rice
1 teaspoon garlic, minced
¼ cup onion, diced
¼ cup green pepper, diced
3 tablespoons oil

2 cups chicken broth
1 cup canned crushed tomatoes
1 tablespoon taco seasoning mix
2 fresh tomatoes, diced

1. In large skillet, sauté rice, garlic, onion and green pepper in hot oil until rice is lightly browned.
2. Add chicken broth, crushed tomatoes, taco seasoning mix and fresh tomatoes. Simmer until liquid is absorbed and rice is tender, about 25 minutes.

Serves 4

STIR-FRIED RICE

1 teaspoon oil	½ cup ham, chicken or pork, diced
1 egg	2 cups cooked rice*
1 green onion	1 tablespoon soy sauce

1. Heat oil in skillet. Add egg and stir-fry until cooked.
2. Add onion and meat. Stir-fry until onion wilts.
3. Add rice and soy sauce. Heat through.

Serves 4

*Leftover rice works great.

"Now join your hands, and with your hands your hearts."
~William Shakespeare

STIR-FRY VEGETABLE MEDLEY

1 medium carrot, cut into matchstick strips
1 celery rib, cut into matchstick strips
1 small onion, sliced thin
1 small bunch broccoli, separated into small pieces
2 tablespoons oil
¼ pound large mushrooms, quartered
¾ teaspoon salt
2 tablespoons water
¼ teaspoon sugar

1. Heat oil in skillet. Stir-fry carrots, celery, onion and broccoli (about 4 minutes.)
2. Add mushrooms, salt, water and sugar.
3. Cover and cook 5 minutes until crisp tender, stirring occasionally.

Serves 4

TWICE BAKED POTATOES

2 medium potatoes
2 tablespoons butter, softened
1/3 cup sour cream
1/4 teaspoon salt
1/8 teaspoon pepper
2/3 cup cheese, grated
1 tablespoon green onion, minced

1. Preheat oven to 400 degrees. Wash and scrub potatoes.
2. Wrap in foil and bake for one hour, or until tender when pierced with fork. Remove from oven.
3. Allow potatoes to cool slightly. Remove foil.
4. Slice each potato in half lengthwise. Carefully scoop center out into a mixing bowl (a melon ball scoop works well). Reserve skins. *The skins will be sturdier if you leave a small rim of potato inside.*
5. Mash potatoes with a potato masher to break up clumps.
6. Add butter, sour cream, salt, pepper and cheese. Add green onion, if desired. Mix well.
7. Scoop potato mixture back into empty potato skins.
8. Bake 350 degrees until hot. Serve with desired toppings.

Makes 4

Suggested Toppings:
Grated cheese
Bacon bits
Parsley flakes
Chives
Buttered crumbs (such as corn flake or cracker)

Buttered crumbs:
1. Mix 1 cup crumbs with 1 tablespoon melted butter.
2. Sprinkle over potatoes and return to oven 3 minutes or until crumbs are crunchy.

Soups

Bean Soup

Broccoli Carrot Soup

Chicken Noodle Soup

Chicken Tortilla Soup

Chili

Clam Chowder

Cream of Carrot & Tomato Soup

Cream of Pumpkin Soup

Creamy Chicken Mushroom Soup

Egg Drop Soup

French Onion Soup

Hearty Beef Soup

Minestrone Soup

Potato Soup

Taco Soup

BEAN SOUP

2 cups dry beans*
½ small onion, optional
1 ham hock**
2 teaspoons salt

1. Look through beans and remove any rocks or bad beans.
2. Place beans in large bowl and cover with several inches of water. Let soak 5 hours or overnight. Drain.
3. Rinse beans and place in heavy pot. Add enough water to cover beans about 2". Cut onion in large pieces and add to beans. Add ham, bacon or salt pork.
4. Bring to a boil, stir well and turn heat to low. When beans are no longer boiling, cover with lid and simmer about 4 hours until beans are very tender. Add salt.
5. Serve with cornbread. (Leftover beans can be used for chili or for refried beans.)

Makes 6 cups

*pinto or white navy beans

**Substitute 4 strips uncooked bacon or 3" piece salt pork, if desired. Remove from beans before serving.

*Caution: Do not leave beans unattended.
If water boils out, beans will burn. Add additional water, if needed.*

Refried Beans:
1 tablespoon oil or bacon grease
2 cups cooked pinto beans
¼ cup liquid from bean soup

1. Heat oil in skillet. Add beans with liquid and mash.
2. Stir and fry beans until desired consistency.

BROCCOLI CARROT SOUP

2 cups fresh broccoli
½ cup carrot, sliced
¼ cup onion, chopped
1½ cups water
1½ teaspoons instant chicken bouillon

1½ cups milk
3 tablespoons flour
½ teaspoon salt
¼ teaspoon pepper
1 tablespoon butter
¾ cup cheese, grated

1. Separate broccoli florets and trim stalks. Combine broccoli florets, carrot, onion, water and bouillon in large saucepan.
2. Cover and cook on medium heat until vegetables are tender, about 8 minutes.
3. With whisk, combine milk, flour, salt and pepper until smooth. Stir into vegetables.
4. Cook on low heat about 10 minutes, stirring occasionally.
5. Add butter and cheese. Stir until melted.

Makes 4 cups

CHICKEN NOODLE SOUP

4 cups chicken broth
¼ teaspoon black pepper
1 large carrot, sliced or grated
1 celery rib, sliced
1½ cups wide egg noodles, uncooked
1½ cups cooked chicken, cut in cubes

1. In large saucepan combine broth, pepper, carrots and celery. Bring to a boil over medium heat. Cook 10 minutes.
2. Stir in noodles and cook 10 minutes, stirring occasionally.
3. Add chicken and heat through.

Makes 5 cups

"How do I love thee? Let me count the ways. I love thee to the depth and breadth and height my soul can reach."
~Elizabeth Barrett Browning

CHICKEN TORTILLA SOUP

2 chicken breast halves
1 tablespoon oil
½ teaspoon garlic, minced
¼ teaspoon ground cumin
½ teaspoon chili powder
4 cups chicken broth
1 (15 ounce) can whole kernel corn, drained
¾ cup mild chunky salsa
8 ounces corn tortilla chips
½ cup cheese, shredded

1. Cut chicken into bite-size cubes. In a large saucepan, sauté chicken in oil until tender.
2. Add garlic, cumin and chili powder. Mix well.
3. Stir in broth, corn and salsa. Simmer 20 minutes.

Makes 6 cups

To serve:
Break up tortilla chips into individual bowls and pour soup over chips. Top with cheese and sour cream.

CHILI

½ pound ground beef
½ small onion, chopped
½ medium green bell pepper, diced
½ (15 ounce) can crushed tomatoes
½ (6 ounce) can tomato paste
1 (4 ounce) can diced green chilies*
¼ small jalapeño, diced*
1 tablespoon chili powder

½ teaspoon cumin
¼ teaspoon dried basil
½ teaspoon garlic, minced
1 cup beef broth
2 cans (15 ounce) beans,
　pinto, white, kidney or black
½ pound pork or chicken, optional

1. Brown ground beef with chopped onion and bell pepper in large saucepan on medium heat. Drain.
2. Add tomatoes, tomato paste, green chilies, jalapeño, chili powder, cumin, basil, garlic and beef broth.
3. Drain beans and add to mixture. Turn heat to low.
4. Cut pork or chicken in small chunks. Heat 1 tablespoon oil in skillet and cook meat until no longer pink in center. Remove from skillet with slotted spoon and add to chili mixture.
5. Simmer, covered, for 1 hour, stirring occasionally.

Makes 6 cups

*Mild Chili: Omit green chilies and jalapeño.

CLAM CHOWDER

1 (6.5 ounce) can minced clams
1 cup potatoes, diced
½ cup onion, diced
½ cup celery, diced
¼ cup butter
¼ cup flour
½ teaspoon salt
⅛ teaspoon white or black pepper
2 cups whole milk
¾ teaspoon sugar

1. Drain clams and reserve liquid.
2. Combine potatoes, onion and celery in a saucepan. Add clam liquid and enough water to cover vegetables.
3. Cover pan and simmer until vegetables are tender, about 15 minutes.
4. In another saucepan, melt butter. Whisk in flour, salt and pepper.
5. Add milk slowly while stirring and cook on low heat until thickened, stirring constantly. Cream soups scorch easily.
6. Mix vegetables and white sauce together.
7. Stir in clams and sugar. Heat through.

Makes 4 cups

CREAM OF CARROT AND TOMATO SOUP

1 pound baby carrots
2 tablespoons butter
1 celery rib, diced
½ cup onion, diced
⅛ teaspoon crushed garlic
¼ teaspoon black pepper
⅛ teaspoon red cayenne pepper
2 tablespoons flour
2 cups water
2 teaspoons chicken bouillon granules
1 (15 ounce) can diced tomatoes
2 cups whole milk

1. Place carrots in saucepan with 3 cups water and bring to a boil. Cover. Reduce heat and simmer 30 minutes. (Do not drain.)
2. Melt butter in large saucepan over medium-high heat. Add celery, onion, garlic, black pepper and red pepper. Sauté until tender.
3. Stir in flour and cook 1 minute, stirring constantly.
4. Gradually stir in 2 cups water and chicken granules. Continue stirring 5 minutes or until slightly thickened.
5. Add carrots with cooking liquid to broth mixture. Stir in tomatoes. Heat, stirring occasionally, 15 minutes. Cool slightly.
6. In blender, process carrot mixture in batches. Blend until smooth, stopping to scrape down sides.
7. Pour into a large saucepan and stir in milk. Cook over low heat, stirring often, 15 minutes or until thoroughly heated.

Makes 6 cups

CREAM OF PUMPKIN SOUP

½ cup onion, minced
2 tablespoons butter
1 tablespoon flour
3 cups chicken broth
1 (15 ounce) can pumpkin

2 tablespoons brown sugar
½ teaspoon salt
⅛ teaspoon pepper
1 cup whole milk
⅛ teaspoon nutmeg

1. Sauté onion in butter until tender. Add flour and stir.
2. Slowly add broth. With whisk stir in pumpkin, brown sugar, salt and pepper until smooth.
3. Heat to boiling. Reduce heat and simmer five minutes.
4. Whisk in milk and nutmeg and cook until heated through.
5. Serve with roasted pumpkin seeds (available in many grocery stores).

Makes 5 cups

CREAMY CHICKEN MUSHROOM SOUP

¼ cup long grain brown rice
 or ¼ cup wild rice*
1 chicken breast half
2 tablespoons butter
2 cups mushrooms, sliced

1 cup celery, chopped
2 tablespoons flour
1 teaspoon salt
1 cup chicken broth
2 cups skim milk

1. Cook rice in 1 cup water about 50 minutes or until liquid is absorbed. (Rice can be prepared the day before and refrigerated in a covered container.)
2. Cut chicken into bite-size pieces. Spray large saucepan with oil and stir fry chicken. Remove from pan and set aside. Clean out pan.
3. Melt butter in same saucepan. Sauté mushrooms and celery.
4. Mix in flour and salt. Slowly add broth. Stir in milk with whisk and cook until soup is thickened.
5. Add cooked chicken and cooked rice. Heat through and serve.

Makes 4 cups

*Precooked wild rice in packets can be purchased in grocery stores.

EGG DROP SOUP

4 cups chicken broth
1 tablespoon cornstarch
1 cup frozen mixed vegetables

1 egg, lightly beaten
1 tablespoon green onion, chopped or fried wonton strips

1. In medium saucepan, whisk cornstarch into broth and heat to a full boil, stirring constantly.
2. Add frozen vegetables and boil 3 minutes.
3. Beat egg with a fork and pour slowly into hot soup. Stir once.
4. Continue cooking 1 minute, and then pour into soup bowls.
5. Garnish with green onion or fried wonton strips, as desired.

Makes 4 cups

"Love is the master key that opens the gates of happiness."
~ Oliver Wendell Holmes

FRENCH ONION SOUP

4 (¾") slices French bread*
2 large yellow onions
1 tablespoon butter
1 tablespoon olive oil
1 tablespoon flour
3 (14 ounce) cans beef broth
2 cups Swiss cheese, grated
8 teaspoons Parmesan cheese

1. Preheat oven to 325 degrees. Bake bread until lightly toasted, about 20 minutes.
2. While bread is toasting, coarsely chop onions.
3. In saucepan, heat butter and olive oil. Add onions and sauté 20 minutes on low heat, stirring occasionally. Stir in flour until blended.
4. Slowly add beef broth. Mix well with a whisk.
5. Add salt, according to taste.
6. Bring to full boil, then simmer 20 minutes.
7. Pour soup into 4 oven safe bowls (1½ cup capacity). Fill almost full.
8. Float slice of toasted French bread on top. Add ½ cup grated Swiss cheese. Repeat with each bowl.
9. Sprinkle 2 teaspoons Parmesan cheese on top of each serving.
10. Preheat oven to 425 degrees. Bake soup for 10 minutes.
11. Turn on broiler unit. Broil on top oven rack until cheese begins to brown. Watch closely.

Makes 6 cups

*Substitute seasoned croutons for bread. After filling bowls with soup, sprinkle croutons generously over top and add Swiss and Parmesan cheeses. Continue with steps 10 and 11.

HEARTY BEEF SOUP

1 pound ground beef or leftover roast beef*
½ small onion, chopped
2 cups beef broth
½ pound baby carrots
4 medium potatoes, peeled and cut in chunks
Salt and pepper, to taste
1½ cups precooked, canned or frozen vegetables of choice, such as tomatoes, green beans or corn

1. In heavy saucepan, brown ground beef and onion. Remove from pan with slotted spoon and set aside. Wipe out pan.
2. Carefully pour beef broth into pan. For thinner soup, add extra broth.
3. Add carrots, potatoes, salt and pepper. Cook low until vegetables are tender, approximately 1 hour. Stir in ground beef mixture.
4. Add any precooked vegetables, if desired, and heat through.

Makes 6 cups

---

*When using leftover cooked roast beef:
1. Cut roast into bite-size chunks. Set aside.
2. In saucepan, sauté onion in oil. Carefully add beef broth.
3. Add carrots, potatoes and other raw vegetables. Cook low until vegetables are tender, about 1 hour.
4. Stir in roast beef and any precooked vegetables of choice.
5. Simmer until well blended and hot.

MINESTRONE SOUP

4 cups water
1 (14.5 ounce) can diced tomatoes
1 cup beef broth
1 cup chicken broth
1 (8 ounce) can tomato sauce
1 celery rib, sliced
2 carrots, sliced
2 tablespoons onion, chopped
1 teaspoon garlic, minced
¼ teaspoon black pepper

1 teaspoon salt
½ teaspoon basil
½ tablespoon parsley
1 teaspoon oregano
1 tablespoon sugar
½ pound sausage, cooked
1 (15 ounce) can green beans
1 (15 ounce) can kidney beans
1 cup macaroni or
   other pasta, uncooked

1. In a large saucepan, combine all ingredients except beans and macaroni.
2. Cook on medium heat 20 minutes.
3. Add beans and macaroni and simmer 30 minutes.

Makes 10 cups

POTATO SOUP

2 cups potatoes, diced
½ cup onion, chopped
1 cup water
½ teaspoon chicken
   bouillon granules
¼ cup butter

¼ cup flour
½ teaspoon salt
⅛ teaspoon pepper
2 cups whole milk
¾ teaspoon sugar

1. Combine potatoes, onion, water and bouillon in large saucepan.*
2. Cover and simmer until potatoes are tender.
3. In a saucepan, melt butter. Slowly add flour, salt and pepper.
4. Whisk in milk and cook on low until thickened, stirring constantly.
5. Combine milk mixture with potato mixture in saucepan. Stir in sugar. Heat through.
6. Garnish with shredded cheese and bacon bits or with strips of red pepper.

Makes 4 cups

*For heartier soup, add ½ cup carrots, celery or other vegetables.

"Have a heart that never hardens, and a temper that never tires, and a touch that never hurts."
~Charles Dickens

TACO SOUP

½ pound ground beef
¼ cup onion, chopped
1 package taco seasoning mix
2 cups water

1 (15 ounce) can kidney beans
1 (15 ounce) can whole kernel corn
1 (14.5 ounce) can diced tomatoes
Corn chips

1. In large saucepan, brown ground beef with onion. Drain.
2. Stir in seasoning mix and water.
3. Drain kidney beans and corn. Add to mixture in pan.
4. Mix in tomatoes. Simmer 20 minutes.
5. To serve: Place corn chips in individual bowls. Add soup.
6. Sprinkle or spoon on toppings, if desired.

Makes 6 cups

Toppings:
Grated cheese
Sour cream
Sliced avocado
Chopped tomatoes
Chopped green onion
Cilantro

Cooking Helps

This section is a guide for those who are new to the tasks of planning menus and shopping lists. The sample menus and sample shopping lists are tools to facilitate the learning curve. Hopefully, after three weeks of practice, the routine will become a habit. The blank menu form and blank shopping list are to be copied for future use when organizing and implementing the home cooking plan from beginning to end. Read "How to Save Money" and "Recycle Leftovers" for further tips on preparing menus and shopping lists. The "Helps" section contains 21 pages of information. It is easy reading with a purpose: the conservation of money, time and trouble.

- **Sample Menu Planners & Shopping Lists** 346
- **Pantry Staples** 354
- **Equivalents** 355
- **Measurements** 356
- **Substitutions** 357
- **Cooking Terms** 358
- **Cooking Tools** 359
- **Organize & Clean** 360
- **Safety Tips** 361
- **Helpful Hints** 362
- **Healthy Eating Tips** 364
- **How to Save Money** 365
- **Recycling Leftovers** 366

SAMPLE MENU PLANNER 1

Week beginning Monday, _____, ending Sunday, _____

L.O. = Leftover   W.W. = Whole Wheat

Breakfast	Lunch	Dinner	Snacks (between meals)
MONDAY: Breakfast Tortillas Grapes Milk	Cottage Cheese with Pineapple W.W. Toast Milk	Stir Fry Beef with Asparagus Rice Milk	Carrot Sticks & Dip Cranberry Juice
TUESDAY: Oatmeal Peaches W.W. Toast Milk	L.O. Stir Fry Applesauce Milk	Chicken Noodle Soup Dinner Rolls Veggies & Dip Cranberry Juice	Bananas Strawberries Yogurt
WEDNESDAY: Bread Pudding made from L.O. Dinner Rolls Orange slices Milk	L.O. Soup Ham Sandwich with Lettuce and Tomato Grape Juice	Southwest Salad Chocolate Pudding Tomato Slices	String Cheese Apple
THURSDAY: Waffles Strawberries and Kiwi Milk	Grilled Cheese Sandwich Tomato Slices Apple Juice	Spaghetti with Meat Sauce Cole Slaw Breadsticks Milk	Deviled Eggs W.W. Toast Grapes
FRIDAY: Egg, Bacon & Cheese on English Muffin Yogurt & Apple Milk	L.O. Spaghetti Cole Slaw Breadsticks Milk	Night Out!	Popcorn Cranberry juice
SATURDAY: Cinnamon French Toast Bananas Milk	Egg Salad Sandwich with Lettuce & Tomato Apple Juice	Chicken and Chilies Raw Veggies Milk	Apple with Peanut Butter Yogurt
SUNDAY: Cereal with Milk W.W. Toast Orange Slices	L.O. Buffet Mandarin Green Salad Milk	Teriyaki Salmon Brown Rice Broccoli Salad Grape Juice	Strawberry Fruit Shake

SHOPPING LIST FOR SAMPLE MENU PLANNER 1

(This list assumes you have the pantry staples.)

Canned & Bottled:
Straw mushrooms (5.95 ounce)
Black beans (15 ounce)
Chili (15 ounce)
Chicken broth (32 ounce)
Diced green chilies (4 ounce)
Applesauce (24 ounce jar)
Mandarin oranges (2 - 11 ounce)
Pineapple chunks (8 ounce)
Lime juice (15 ounce)

Packaged:
Wide egg noodles (12 ounce)
Brown rice (28 ounce bag)
Cereal (whole grain)
Pudding/pie filling mix (1)
Raisins (12 ounce bag)
Sliced almonds (6 ounce bag)
Sunflower kernels, roasted & salted (snack size bag)
Popcorn

Produce:
Apples (6)
Bananas (6)
Grapes (1 large bunch)
Kiwi (2)
Oranges (4)
Peaches (2)
Strawberries (1 quart)
Asparagus (1 bunch)
Avocado (1)
Onion (1 bunch green, 1 red)
Tomatoes (4)
Broccoli (1 bunch - 2 cups)
Cabbage (1 small head)
Carrots (2 pound bag)
Celery (1 stalk)
Cilantro (1 bunch)
Tomatillos (3)
Lettuce (1 iceberg, 1 romaine)

Dairy:
Cottage cheese (16 ounce)
Buttermilk (½ pint)
Yogurt (6)
String cheese (4 sticks)
Eggs

Meat:
Ribeye steak (¾ pound)
Chicken breast halves (6)
Salmon (2 small fillets)
Ground beef (½ pound)
Deli ham (4 sandwich slices)
Bacon (1 pound)

Bakery:
Whole wheat bread (1 loaf)
English muffins (6 whole grain)
Flour tortillas (10"- package of 8)

Frozen:
Juices (12 ounce - apple, cranberry, grape)
Ice cream (½ gallon)

Miscellaneous:
Liquid Dish Soap

SAMPLE MENU PLANNER 2

Week beginning Monday,_____,ending Sunday,_____

L.O.=Leftover W.W.=Whole Wheat

Breakfast	Lunch	Dinner	Snacks (between meals)
MONDAY: Banana Slices Waffles with Brown Sugar Topping Milk	Club Sandwich Chips Cranberry Juice	Fried Chicken Steak Baked Potato Green Salad with Dressing Milk	Orange Slices Celery Sticks
TUESDAY: Scrambled Eggs Bacon Hash Browns Pancake Orange Juice	Spinach Salad with Strawberries & Pecans Milk	Bean Soup Cornbread Raw Veggies Milk	Apple with Peanut Butter String Cheese
WEDNESDAY: Sliced Peaches Oatmeal English Muffin Milk	L.O. Soup Cornbread Raw Veggies Milk	BBQ Chicken Salad French Bread Cranberry Juice	Orange Smoothie Oatmeal Raisin Cookie
THURSDAY: Spinach with Eggs W.W. Toast Apple Juice	L.O. BBQ Salad Crackers Milk	Lasagna Green beans L.O. French Bread Cranberry Juice	String Cheese W.W. toast with Peanut Butter
FRIDAY: Cold Cereal with Milk Strawberries W.W. Toast with Peanut Butter	L.O. Lasagna Green Beans W.W. Toast Milk	Lettuce Wedge Salad Carrot & Tomato Soup English Muffin	Yogurt Oatmeal Raisin Cookie
SATURDAY: Biscuits and Gravy Apple Slices Milk	L.O. Soup W.W. Toast String Cheese	Pork Chops Celery stuffed with 'Jar' Cheese Baked Sweet Potato Milk	Orange Smoothie Corn Chips & Salsa
SUNDAY: Canned Pears Omelet (L.O. veggies) Yogurt	Tuna Sandwich Vegetable Soup Fruit Salad Apple Juice	Pot Roast Mashed Potatoes with Gravy Peas and Carrots Milk	String Cheese Apple

SHOPPING LIST FOR SAMPLE MENU PLANNER 2

(This list assumes you have the pantry staples and some items leftover from previous week.)

Canned & Bottled:
Sliced peaches (15 ounce)
Pear halves (15 ounce)
Green beans (14.5 ounce)
Diced green chilies (4 ounce)
Tuna (6 ounce)
Vegetable soup (1)
BBQ sauce (16 ounce)
Soft cheese (5 ounce jar)

Packaged:
Cornmeal
Lasagna noodles (8 ounce)
Pecans (6 ounce)
Dry beans (16 ounce bag - pinto or white navy)
Dry bread crumbs (15 ounce)
Chips (10 ounce bag)
Dried cranberries (6 ounce bag)

Produce:
Bananas (4)
Oranges (4)
Apples (4)
Strawberries (1 quart)
Kiwi (2)
Sweet potatoes or yams (2 medium)
Green bell pepper (1)
Avocado (1)
Baby carrots (2 - 1 pound bags)
Baby spinach (6 ounce)
1 small jalapeño
1 bag greens (with shredded carrots and purple cabbage)

Dairy:
Yogurt (6)
String cheese (8)
Cheese slices (6 - white & yellow)
Eggs

Meat:
Chicken breast halves (4)
Ground beef (1 pound)
Pork chops (2)
Beef pot roast (3 pounds)
Deli turkey & ham (6 slices each)
Bulk sausage (½ pound)
Ham hock (1) or thick bacon (½ pound)

Bakery:
Whole wheat bread (1 loaf)

Frozen:
Juices (12 ounce - cranberry, orange, apple)
Peas and carrots (10 ounce)

Miscellaneous:
Rubber gloves

SAMPLE MENU PLANNER 3

Week beginning Monday,_____,ending Sunday,_____

L.O.=Leftover W.W.=Whole Wheat

Breakfast	Lunch	Dinner	Snacks (between meals)
MONDAY: Blueberry Muffins Banana Milk	Deviled Eggs Raw Veggies & Dip W.W. Bread Milk	Chimichangas from L.O. Pot Roast Lettuce & Tomatoes Sour Cream Apple Juice	Grapes Cream Cheese and Crackers
TUESDAY: Fried Egg and Ham Sandwich Orange Slices Milk	L.O. Chimichangas Apple Milk	Cashew Chicken Stir-Fry Rice Kiwi Cranberry juice	Graham Crackers Milk
WEDNESDAY: Bagel with Cream Cheese Grapes Milk	L.O. Cashew Chicken Rice Milk	Clam Chowder Raw Veggies Garlic Cheese Toast Apple Juice	Orange Gingersnap Cookies Milk
THURSDAY: Puff Pancake with Raspberries Milk	Chili Dogs Potato Salad L.O. Blueberry Muffins Milk	Taco Soup Corn Chips/Avocado* Green Salad Cranberry Juice	Cottage Cheese with Mandarin Oranges W.W. Toast
FRIDAY: Veggie Omelet Orange Slices Milk	L.O. Clam Chowder Apple Slices Toast	Night Out!	Carrots Cheese and Crackers
SATURDAY: French Toast Applesauce Milk	Grilled Cheese Sandwich Tomato Soup Orange	California Wrap with Grilled Chicken Milk	Popcorn Apple Slices
SUNDAY: Cold Cereal with Banana W.W. Toast Milk	Patty Melt Cheese Fries Orange Shake	Pasta Chicken Salad with Mango & Avocado W.W. Toast Milk	Kiwi Gingersnap Cookies

*When using half an avocado, leave peel on reserved half. Spread lemon juice on cut side, place in small baggie and store in refrigerator. If fruit darkens, scrape off top layer.

SHOPPING LIST FOR SAMPLE MENU PLANNER 3

(This list assumes you have the pantry staples and some items leftover from previous weeks.)

Canned & Bottled:
Clams (6.5 ounce)
Whole kernel corn (15 ounce)
Kidney beans (15 ounce)
Diced tomatoes (14.5 ounce)
Mandarin oranges (11 ounce)
Tomato soup (10¾ ounce)
Pineapple tidbits (8 ounce)

Packaged:
Graham crackers (14 ounce)
Corn chips (10 ounce)
Cashews (10 ounce)

Produce:
Bananas (6)
Grapes (1 large bunch)
Oranges (4)
Mango (1)
Kiwi (2)
Raspberries (1 pint)
Apples (4)
Carrots (2 pounds)
Broccoli (1 bunch)
Snow peas (¼ pound)
Lettuce (1 head, leafy)
Tomatoes (2)
Avocado (2)

Dairy:
Cottage cheese (16 ounce)
Cream cheese (8 ounce tub)
Deli cheese (6 thin slices)
Eggs

Meat:
Hot dogs (fat free package of 8)
Ground beef (1½ pounds)
Chicken breast halves (4)
Shaved deli ham (8 ounce)

Bakery:
French bread (1 loaf)
Bagels (2)
Hot dog buns (package of 8)
Tortillas (10"- package of 8)

Frozen:
Juices (12 ounce - apple, cranberry, grape)
Ice cream (½ gallon)
Orange sherbet (1 pound package)

Miscellaneous:
Toothpaste
Light bulbs

MENU PLANNER

Week beginning Monday,_____,ending Sunday,_____

Breakfast	Lunch	Dinner	Snacks (between meals)
MONDAY:			
TUESDAY:			
WEDNESDAY:			
THURSDAY:			
FRIDAY:			
SATURDAY:			
SUNDAY:			

SHOPPING LIST

Canned & Bottled:	Meat:
Packaged:	Bakery:
Produce:	Frozen:
Dairy:	Miscellaneous:

PANTRY STAPLES

Take inventory weekly and re-stock pantry as needed.

Bottled and Canned Goods:
Black Olives
Canned Evaporated Milk
Canned Tomatoes
Corn Syrup
Cream of Chicken Soup
Cream of Mushroom Soup
Honey
Ketchup
Lemon Juice
Mayonnaise
Molasses
Mustard
Olive Oil
Peanut Butter
Pickles/Pickle Relish
Sesame Oil
Shortening
Soy Sauce
Tomato Paste
Tomato Sauce
Vegetable Oil
Vinegar (white, apple cider)
Worcestershire Sauce

Dry ingredients:
Baking Cocoa
Baking Powder
Baking Soda
Brown Sugar
Cornstarch
Oatmeal
Powdered Sugar
Sugar
White Flour
Whole Wheat Flour
Yeast

Flavorings:
Almond Extract
Lemon Extract
Maple Extract
Vanilla Extract

Food Coloring:
Small 4 color pack

Instant Mix Ingredients:
Bouillon Granules
  (chicken/beef)
Potato Flakes
Powdered Milk

Paper Products:
Aluminum Foil
Food Storage Bags
Napkins
Paper Cups
Paper Plates
Paper Towels
Plastic Wrap
Wax Paper

Produce and Starch:
Onions
Potatoes
Rice
Saltine Crackers
Spaghetti Pasta

Refrigerator Staples:
Bottled Garlic
Bottled Ginger

Butter
Cheddar Cheese
Eggs
Milk
Parmesan Cheese
Salsa
Sour Cream

Seasonings & Spices:
Basil
Black Pepper
Chili Powder
Cinnamon
Cream of Tartar
Cumin
Curry Powder
Dill Weed
Dry Mustard
Garlic Powder
Garlic Salt
Ginger
Minced Onion
Nutmeg
Oregano
Paprika
Parsley flakes
Poppy Seeds
Red Pepper (cayenne)
Salt & Seasoned Salt
Spaghetti Sauce packets
Taco Seasoning packets
Tarragon
Ranch Dressing packets
French Onion Soup packets

EQUIVALENTS

1 small onion	=	1 cup chopped onion
1 medium tomato	=	1 cup chopped tomato
1 large rib celery	=	½ cup diced celery
1 large clove garlic	=	1 teaspoon chopped garlic
4 medium potatoes	=	4 cups sliced raw potatoes
1 medium banana	=	½ cup mashed banana
1 pint fresh strawberries	=	2 cups sliced strawberries
1 medium lemon	=	3 tablespoons lemon juice or 2 teaspoons lemon zest
1 medium orange	=	¼ cup orange juice or 4 teaspoons orange zest
1 medium apple	=	1 cup grated apple
1 small apple	=	1 cup sliced apples
2 slices fresh bread	=	1 cup bread crumbs
8 ounces firm cheese	=	2 cups shredded cheese
1 cup uncooked rice	=	3 cups cooked rice
½ cup heavy cream	=	1 cup whipped cream
1 (12 ounce) can evaporated milk	=	1½ cups evaporated milk
1 chicken breast half	=	1 cup chopped chicken

Some listed amounts are approximate. They will vary according to your defintion of small, medium or large.

MEASUREMENTS

Cup	Ounces	Tablespoons	Teaspoons
1 cup	8 ounces	16 tablespoons	48 teaspoons
¾ cup	6 ounces	12 tablespoons	36 teaspoons
½ cup	4 ounces	8 tablespoons	24 teaspoons
¼ cup	2 ounces	4 tablespoons	12 teaspoons
1/8 cup	1 ounce	2 tablespoons	6 teaspoons
1/16 cup	½ ounce	1 tablespoon	3 teaspoons

2 cups = 1 pint

4 cups (2 pints) = 1 quart

4 quarts (liquid) = 1 gallon

16 ounces (solid) = 1 pound

8 quarts (solid) = 1 peck

4 pecks = 1 bushel

Use proper measuring cups for liquid and dry ingredients.

SUBSTITUTIONS

Ingredient	Amount	Substitute
Baking mix	3 cups	3 cups flour, 1 tablespoon plus 2 teaspoons baking powder, 1½ teaspoons salt. Mix together and cut in 2/3 cup shortening.
Bread crumbs	¼ cup	¼ cup finely crushed cracker or corn flake crumbs
Broth (chicken or beef)	1 cup	1 teaspoon chicken or beef bouillon granules (or 1 cube) dissolved in 1 cup boiling water
Buttermilk	1 cup	1 cup milk plus 1 tablespoon lemon juice or white vinegar
Cake flour	1 cup	1 cup all purpose flour minus 2 tablespoons
Dry mustard	1 teaspoon	1 tablespoon prepared mustard
Garlic	1 clove	1 teaspoon garlic powder or 1 teaspoon bottled garlic
Juice of lemon	1 medium lemon	3 tablespoons bottled lemon juice
Juice of orange	1 medium orange	¼ cup orange juice
Lemon peel	1 teaspoon	½ teaspoon lemon extract
Onion	1 small	1 teaspoon onion powder or 1 tablespoon minced dried onion
Red pepper sauce	3 or 4 drops	1/8 teaspoon ground red pepper (cayenne)
Semisweet baking chocolate	1 ounce	1 ounce unsweetened baking chocolate plus 1 tablespoon sugar
Unsweetened baking chocolate	1 ounce	3 tablespoons baking cocoa plus 1 tablespoon shortening or margarine
Whole Milk	1 cup	½ cup evaporated milk plus ½ cup water

COOKING TERMS

Baste: To brush or spoon a liquid or other moist ingredient over food during cooking.

Beat: To stir vigorously with electric mixer, wire whisk or spoon. This incorporates air into the mixture.

Bias Slice: To slice a food crosswise at a 45 degree angle.

Blend: To combine two or more ingredients thoroughly.

Boil: To maintain liquid at its boiling point. Liquid will be bubbling vigorously.

Bread: To coat with bread crumbs or other types of ground grains.

Chill: Cool in refrigerator.

Chop: To cut food into small pieces, about ½ inch.

Cream: To combine softened fat thoroughly with sugar.

Cut in: (shortening or butter) To mix into dry ingredients using a pastry blender or two kitchen knives, until the fat is reduced to small pieces similar in size to peas.

Dice: To cut food into small pieces, about ¼ inch.

Dust: To sprinkle lightly with flour or sugar.

Finely chop: Another term for dice.

Fold in: Add gently, often with a spatula or wooden spoon, with as little stirring as possible.

Fry: To cook in hot fat.

Grate: To cut into small strips with hand grater or use food processor with grating blade.

Grease and flour pan: To coat inside of pan with shortening until entire surface is lightly covered, using fingers or plastic wrap. To flour, spoon 1 tablespoon flour on greased pan. Turn pan in all directions while tapping bottom and sides of pan to distribute flour. Turn pan over sink and tap to remove excess flour.

Julienne: (vegetables) To cut into very thin strips.

Knead: (dough) To turn dough repeatedly while folding it over itself with the heel of your hand (this should be done on a lightly floured board or lightly floured clean/dry counter) or with dough hook on mixer to develop the gluten, or structure, of the dough.

Mince: To chop or cut into very fine pieces, smaller than diced.

Sauté: To briefly pan fry in small amount of fat while stirring constantly.

Scald: To heat liquid a little below boiling point. Small bubbles will form around edges.

Scant: Slightly less than the actual measure.

Shred: (cheese) To cut into strips using a hand grater or grating blade on food processor.

Shred with fork: (meat or spaghetti squash) Using two forks back to back, pull meat or squash into small slivers.

Simmer: To maintain the temperature of food at almost boiling.

Whip: To use wire whisk or electric mixer and combine ingredients at high speed.

COOKING TOOLS

ORGANIZE & CLEAN

Getting Organized

- Organize the kitchen:
  - Place 'like' utensils and bowls together.
  - Place dishtowels near the sink, baking pans in the drawer under the oven, pots and pans near the stovetop, plates and silverware near the table, plastic wrap near the microwave and hot pads near the stove.
  - Establish a baking center: Place ingredients for baking in same location, such as flour, sugar, baking cocoa, shortening, oil, baking powder, baking soda, salt and spices. Place baking utensils together, such as measuring cups, measuring spoons, dough roller, whisks, spatulas, pastry blender and wooden spoons.

- Cooking: Read recipe through and gather utensils, bowls, pots or pans and ingredients. As you add each ingredient, put it away to prevent adding it twice. This will make kitchen cleanup quicker.

Cleaning Tips

- Wash the dishes. It's easiest to wash them as they are used.
  - Dishwasher: Rinse dirty dishes and place inside immediately after use.
  - No dishwasher: A sink full of hot soapy water makes quick cleanup. This can be accomplished in a matter of minutes.
  - Pots and pans: Wash immediately after using or fill with water to soak.
  - After the meal, have everyone carry their own dishes to the sink, and wash them or place in the dishwasher . . . a good exercise in personal responsibility!

- Clean off counters.
  - Wipe off any surfaces where there are food splatters.
  - Using hot soapy water and a clean dish cloth, wipe off all countertops and appliances that were used during cooking.

- Clean the floor.
  - Sweep first and mop up spills and splatters, if necessary.
  - Sometimes you only need a quick swipe with a cleaning rag or paper towel.

- Cleaning is easiest when done regularly. Leaving the mess until later makes it twice the work and twice the dread. You waste time trying to find things when you allow your kitchen to become cluttered and dirty.

- Use an old toothbrush or toothpick to clean grooves, such as in stove or around sink.

- Immediately after rolling dough, wipe rolling pin and board clean with a paper towel.

- For oven spillovers: Sprinkle with salt and remove with spatula. Wipe with damp sponge.

- Wash dishcloths, dishtowels and sponges often – leaving dirty, moist cloths creates an environment for harmful bacteria.

SAFETY TIPS

Safety Tips (Fire)

1. To avoid fires, never leave cooking unattended.
2. If there is a fire on top of the stove, TURN OFF THE STOVE.
3. Smother a grease fire by covering with lid; never pour water on it.
4. If there is a fire in the oven, LEAVE DOOR SHUT and turn off oven.
5. To prevent severe burns, never attempt to carry boiling hot oil or flaming pans.
6. Baking soda will smother most fires, except burning wax.
7. Purchase a fire extinguisher and know how to use it.
8. If flames do not go out immediately, get out of the house and call 911.

Safety Tips (Procedure)

1. Turn pot handles toward back of stove.
2. To prevent burns, use oven mitts. Do not use 'wet' oven mitts when handling hot pans. Do not lift the cover from a hot pan or bowl without an oven mitt.
3. Unplug mixer before removing beaters.
4. Turn knife blades down when loading dishwasher. Do not drop sharp knives into dishwater. Beneath the soapy water, they become invisible. Place glassware in the water carefully to avoid the hazard of broken glass.

Safety Tips (Cooking with Oil)

1. To prevent splattering, dry hands before working over hot oil.
2. Use long handled tongs to remove food from hot oil.
3. Do not fill cooking pot more than ½ full with oil to prevent boil over.
4. Do not cover hot oil. When leaving the room for any reason while cooking with oil, turn off the stove.
5. Never pour hot oil into a container of any kind. Allow oil to cool first.

Safe Food Handling

1. Before cooking, wash hands well with soap and water.
2. Sanitize wooden and plastic cutting boards by washing with bleach water (1/3 cup bleach in 1 quart water), especially after cutting raw meat. This is also a good solution for sanitizing the drain where harmful bacteria can grow. Wear rubber gloves.
3. After handling raw meat, fish, poultry or eggs, wash hands. Wash work surfaces with hot, soapy water and sanitize before using for other foods.
4. Thaw frozen meats in refrigerator or under cold running water.
5. Refrigerate perishable food within 2 hours of cooking.
6. Store meat, fish and poultry in well-sealed packages to prevent leakage onto other foods.
7. Keep refrigerator temperature 40 degrees Fahrenheit; freezer temperature 0 degrees Fahrenheit.
8. Keep cold food cold and hot food hot to avoid the growth of dangerous bacteria that cause food poisoning.

HELPFUL HINTS

Baking:

- Soften butter at room temperature. Quick-soften: Leave cold butter in paper and microwave 10 seconds or slightly longer if needed. Be careful not to allow butter to melt in center.

- Use large eggs for baking. Always store eggs in refrigerator; they will keep longer if stored in original carton. If recipe calls for eggs at room temperature, place eggs (in shells) in warm water for a few minutes.

- To melt chocolate: Chop into pieces (or use chocolate chips). Place in microwave safe bowl (do not cover) and microwave full power 30 seconds. Stir and repeat until melted. To melt on stove-top, place half the chocolate in heavy saucepan and heat low until chocolate is melted. Remove from heat and stir in remaining chocolate until melted.

- For easier biscuits, roll dough in rectangle and cut in squares.

- Pastry recipes work best if whole milk is used.

- When making cookies, line your cookie sheet with parchment paper for even baking and easy clean up.

- To test doneness of cake, insert toothpick into center of cake. If it comes out clean or with only a few crumbs, it is done. Also, the edges will begin to pull away from sides of pan.

- When a recipe calls for sifted ingredients, use sifter or mix well with a whisk.

- To save energy and ensure accurate baking, use oven window rather than opening oven to check on baked goods.

- Use active dry yeast (check expiration date; baked goods will not rise properly if old yeast is used). Good yeast will increase in size or become foamy when dissolved in warm water. Do not dissolve in hot water as it can kill the yeast.

- Keep several flour-sack dishcloths available to be used only for baking.

- When flour is listed, use all-purpose; for sugar, use granulated, unless otherwise specified. (For best results use bread flour when making bread.)

Serving:

- To cut meringue on pie, butter the knife on both sides.

- Use thin blade knife to cut cheesecake. Wipe knife between cuts.

- Serve cheese at room temperature. Cheese can be frozen but it will affect the flavor and texture. If frozen, use in recipes that call for melted cheese.

- For best chocolate curls, use white or milk chocolate as they are softer. Unwrap and warm candy bar a few seconds in microwave. Use a potato peeler and run down side of chocolate bar to make curls.

- Dip ice cream scoop in hot water for easier scooping.

Miscellaneous:

- For added flavor, toast nuts before adding to a recipe. (To toast nuts, place in single layer on ungreased cookie sheet. Bake 350 degrees about 5 to 10 minutes, stirring occasionally.)

- Ziploc bags work great for marinating.

- Use a salad spinner to create a crisp salad rather than a soggy one.

- Liquids will boil faster and food will cook faster if you put a lid on the pan. (Do not cover hot oil.)

- To improve cooking, note changes in recipes that would better suit your taste.

- Invest in good quality cookware. Food will burn more easily in pots and pans that are too thin. Cheap nonstick pans can peel and leave unappetizing residue in your food.

- Favorite recipes are quick to assemble when chicken, rice, dressings, etc. are cooked or mixed in advance and refrigerated until needed.

HEALTHY EATING TIPS

1. Limit fats. Measure the amount of fats used in recipes. At 100 calories per tablespoon, measuring matters!

2. When possible, cut down the salt in recipes. If you often eat salty fried foods, such as chips, you will consume empty calories which will also increase your thirst and water retention.

3. Limit meat to small portions. Substitute some vegetable dishes for meat in your menu.

4. Eat fiber daily in the form of whole grains and beans, fresh fruits and vegetables. When possible, leave skins on fruits and vegetables to retain nutrients.

5. Substitute low fat or nonfat ingredients in recipes when possible: skim milk, nonfat sour cream, nonfat half and half, low or nonfat canned soup. However, some recipes such as pudding and pastry will not give the desired results with less fat. For successful baking, do not use soft tub margarine.

6. Limit refined sugars, especially soda, candy, cookies and cakes. If you eat these foods daily, you are curbing your appetite for "real" food and your health will suffer. Make dessert an "occasion" that happens once or twice a week.

7. Drink your milk. Mom was right! It will make your bones "fat" and strong. If you are lactose intolerant, lactose free milks can be purchased in grocery stores. Yogurt is also a good choice for calcium.

8. Eat regular meals with healthy snacks between meals. An apple, nuts or carrot sticks make excellent snacks when you are on the run. Plan ahead by keeping healthy snacks and water in your car in case you become hungry and thirsty far from home.

9. Avoid eating late at night. It is best to consume the majority of your calories earlier in the day.

10. Food is your friend. Unless certain medical conditions prevent it, you can eat what you like if moderation is used in your choices. Eat foods that will rebuild cells and protect your immune system! Good health is your most valuable resource and one of the major keys to a happy and productive life.

HOW TO SAVE MONEY

1. Inventory your pantry, refrigerator and freezer weekly and plan a MENU* that makes use of as many leftovers as possible.

2. Prepare a SHOPPING LIST* to avoid impulse buying. Eat before shopping. If you are hungry, you are more likely to exceed your budget.

3. Watch for coupons and sales. When your budget will allow, buy a few extra sale items that you use most often.

4. Cook on a regular basis. You cannot save money if you shop for a week's groceries and waste half of them by eating out 4 nights a week.

5. Conserve the resources you have.

Tips to keep food fresh longer and avoid waste:

- Shortening and other foods, such as peanut butter, can become rancid if left on the shelf too long. Store them in the refrigerator to prolong shelf life.
- Shelled nuts stay fresh longer if stored in freezer bags in the freezer.
- To reconstitute hard raisins, place in a saucepan and cover with cold water. Bring to a boil. Remove from heat and let stand a few minutes. Drain well.
- "Save the Pudding": If pudding scorches or sticks, immediately pour into another pan without scraping the bottom and continue to cook. Also works when cooking sauces unless it is burned badly enough to affect the taste.
- Strain used (cooled) cooking oil through a wire mesh strainer and store in a sealable plastic bottle or glass jar for future use. The oil can be reused several times.
- To prevent moldy bread, divide the loaf and place in freezer bags. Store in freezer.
- Soak limp veggies (celery, carrots, etc.) in ice water to crisp.
- Celery will stay crisp for several weeks when wrapped in foil and stored in the refrigerator.
- Yeast lasts longer if stored in the refrigerator. It will keep up to one year if placed in a tightly sealed container in the freezer. (There is usually an expiration date stamped on the package.)
- Simple things such as sealing the bread bag or putting lids on jars can prevent waste by keeping food fresh longer.

*See blank menu forms and shopping lists.

RECYLING LEFTOVERS

1. Place leftover food in freezer containers or plastic freezer bags and freeze. (Label containers with date and name of food inside.)

2. Add leftover cooked rice or cooked noodles to soups, salads or stir fry dishes.

3. Cool leftover pancakes, waffles or French toast and freeze in single layers. When frozen, place in freezer bags and return to freezer. Reheat in toaster.

4. Leftover fresh veggies from veggie tray can be used in soups, stews, omelets or casseroles. Cut leftover fresh corn off the cob and store in plastic container in refrigerator or freezer. Mix with butter and salt and use as a side dish or add to soup or casseroles.

5. Use leftover beef or chicken in salads, pot pies, casseroles, stir fry, sandwiches or wraps. Leftover beef roast, pork or meatloaf can be diced and added to spaghetti sauce. For a quick breakfast, add leftover meat to scrambled eggs or hash browns.

6. Cut stale bread into cubes or process into crumbs and store in freezer.

7. Raw egg whites can be frozen in small plastic freezer bag or container for later use.

8. Use leftover mashed potatoes to make potato rolls or as a topping for casseroles.

9. To recycle hardened brown sugar, place a slice of white bread in the bag and seal. It will soften the sugar. This tip also freshens cookies made with brown sugar.

10. Freeze leftover cookies or cake in small containers to pack in lunches.

Frozen foods:
Some foods can be frozen longer than others before the quality of the food deteriorates. (Check your freezer guide for suggested freezing times.) For example, baked goods will deteriorate more quickly than meat.

Refrigerated foods:
To ensure freshness, check expiration dates on refrigerated foods.
Be especially cautious of lunch meats. (Discard if they are outdated or have a bad odor.) Some items such as sour cream and buttermilk can last up to a month or more after expiration. If mold is present, discard the item. If it looks and smells fresh, it can be used. Cheese is still edible if moldy spots are cut from it.

Index

Apple Crisp, 129
Apple Dip, 7
Apple Harvest Cake, 109
Apple Pie, 131
Artichoke Dip, 9
Asian Dipping Sauce, 21
Baked Beans, 279
Baked Meringue, 133
Baked Potatoes, 281
Banana Pudding, 135
BBQ Chicken Salad, 227
BBQ Pork Sandwiches, 259
Bean Soup, 315
Berry Cobbler, 137
Berry Topping, 145
Biscuits, 47
Biscuits and Gravy, 77
Blueberry Muffins, 79
Bread Pudding, 81
Breadsticks, 57
Breakfast Tortillas, 83
Broccoli Carrot Soup, 317
Broccoli Salad, 229
Brownies, 153
Buttermilk Banana Bread, 49
Buttermilk Banana Muffins, 49
Butters:
   Brown Sugar Butter, 281
   Cinnamon Honey Butter, 69
   Honey Butter, 69
   Maple Butter, 281
   Orange Honey Butter, 69
   Raspberry Butter, 69
   Strawberry Butter, 63

California Wrap, 261
Caramel Apple Sundaes, 129
Carrot Casserole, 283
Cashew Chicken, 189
Cheddar Fries, 285
Cheese Ball, 11
Cheese Biscuits, 51
Cheesecake, 139
Cherry Chocolate Cake, 111
Chicken Alfredo, 297
Chicken and Broccoli, 191
Chicken and Chilies, 193
Chicken Chunks, 13
Chicken Cordon Bleu, 195
Chicken Cutlets, 197
Chicken Noodle Soup, 319
Chicken Parmesan, 205
Chicken Pasta Salad with Fruit, 231
Chicken Pockets, 199
Chicken Pot Pie, 201
Chicken Salad Sandwiches, 263
Chicken Tortilla Soup, 321
Chili, 323
Chili Dogs, 265
Chimichangas, 203
Chocolate Cake, 113
Chocolate Chip Cookies, 155
Chocolate Dessert, 141
Chocolate Fondant, 127
Christmas Wreaths, 157
Cinnamon Swirl Bread, 85
Cinnamon French Toast, 85
Clam Chowder, 325
Club Sandwich, 267
Cobb Salad for Two, 233
Cole Slaw, 235
Company Potatoes, 287
Cookie Frosting, 159
Cornbread, 53
Cornbread Muffins, 53
Country Potato Salad, 237
Cream Cheese Carrot Cake, 115
Cream of Carrot and Tomato Soup, 327
Cream of Pumpkin Soup, 329
Creamy Chicken Mushroom Soup, 331
Creamy Mashed Potatoes, 288
Crepes, 87
Crunchy Salad, 239

Dessert Toppings:
   Hot Fudge Sauce, 145

    Strawberry Topping, 145
Deviled Eggs, 289
Dinner Rolls, 55
Dips:
    Apple Dip, 7
    Artichoke Dip, 9
    Asian Dip, 21
    Fruit Dip, 17
    Guacamole Dip, 19
    Ranch Dill Dip, 33
    Spinach Artichoke Dip, 9
    Taco Platter Dip, 31

Egg Drop Soup, 333
Egg Rolls, 15
Egg Salad Sandwich, 269
Family Favorite Cake, 117
French Bread, 57
French Dip Sandwich, 271
French Onion Soup, 335
Fried Cauliflower, 291
Fried Chicken Steak, 205
Frostings:
    Caramel Frosting, 123
    Chocolate Buttercream, 113
    Chocolate Fondant, 127
    Chocolate Frosting, 169
    Coconut Pecan Frosting, 121
    Cookie Frosting, 159
    Cream Cheese Frosting, 115
    Fudge Frosting, 111
    Magic Frosting, 117
    White Fondant,127
    White Wedding Cake Frosting, 126
Fruit Dip, 17
Fruit Nut Loaf, 59
Fruit Parfait, 143
Fruit Shakes, 35

Gingerbread Boys, 161
Gingersnap Cookies, 163
Glazed Carrots, 293

Graham Cracker Crust, 139
Green Beans with Slivered Almonds, 295
Guacamole Dip, 19
Halloween Peanut Butter Fingers, 165
Hash Browns, 89
Hearty Beef Soup, 337
Hearty Cheese Ball, 11
Homemade Doughnuts, 91
Homemade Syrup, 93
Hot Fudge Topping, 145
Ice Cream Pie, 145

Key Lime Pie, 147
Lasagna, 207
Lemon Bars, 167
Lemon Cake, 119
Lettuce Wedge Salad, 241
Lettuce Wraps, 21
Mandarin Green Salad, 243
Manicotti, 209
Marshmallow Brownies, 169
Meatballs, 23
Mexican Haystacks, 211
Mild Beef Enchiladas, 213
Minestrone Soup, 339
Monterey Chicken Croissants, 273
Mornay Suance, 195
Mozzarella Tomato Salad, 245

No Bake Chocolate Cookies, 171
Oatmeal Cake, 121
Oatmeal Raisin Cookies, 173
Orange Smoothie, 37
Overnight Breakfast Casserole, 95

Pancakes, 97
Party Root Beer, 39
Pasta Alfredo, 297
Pasta Salad with Veggies, 247

Patty Melt, 275
Peanut Butter Bars, 175
Peanut Butter Cookies, 177
Peanut Butter Kiss Cookies, 177
Pigs in Blankets, 25
Platter Salad, 249
Poppy Seed Bread, 61
Pot Roast, 215
Potato Rolls, 63
Potato Salad, 251
Potato Soup, 341
Puff Pancake, 99
Pumpkin Chocolate Chip Bread, 65
Pumpkin Chocolate Chip Muffins, 65

Quesadilla, 27
Quick Banana Bread, 67
Rainbow Freeze, 41
Raspberry Thumbprints, 179
Refried Beans, 315
Rice Pilaf, 299
Round Steak with Gravy, 217

Salad Dressings:
   Chunky Bleu Cheese Dressing, 241
   Cilantro Buttermilk Dressing, 253
   Creamy Salad Dressing, 229
   Light Poppy Seed Dressing, 227
   Lime Tarragon Salad Dressing, 231
   Oil Vinegar Dressing, 243
   Poppy Seed Dressing, 249
   Thousand Island Dressing, 233
Salsa, 29
Sauces:
   Asian Dipping Sauce, 21
   Barbecue Sauce, 23
   BBQ Sauce, 259
   Butter Sauce, 109
   Caramel Sauce, 109
   Easy Gravy, 217
   Fry Sauce, 285
   Hot Wing Sauce, 13

   Mornay Sauce, 195
   Mustard Sauce, 13
   Sweet and Sour Sauce, 23
   Teriyaki Sauce, 223
Sausage Gravy, 77
Sautéed Mushrooms, 301
Scones, 69
Simple Wassail, 43
Snickerdoodles, 181
Sour Cream Cake, 123
Southwest Salad, 253
Spaghetti Squash, 303
Spaghetti with Meat Sauce, 219
Spanish Rice, 305
Spinach Artichoke Dip, 9
Spinach Salad, 255
Spinach with Eggs, 101
Stir-Fried Rice, 307
Stir-Fry Beef, 221
Stir-Fry Vegetable Medley, 309
Sugar Cookies, 183

Taco Platter Dip, 31
Taco Soup, 343
Teriyaki Grill, 223
Trifle, 149
Twice Baked Potatoes, 311
Veggie Omelet, 103
Veggie Tray and Dip, 33
Waffles, 105
Wassail, Simple, 43
Wheat Bread, 71
White Bread, 73
White Wedding Cake, 125
White Wedding Cookies, 185
White Wedding Cake Frosting, 126
White Wedding Fondant, 127

NOTES

372

NOTES

374

NOTES

NOTES

378